Globalization and Voices from Indian Practitioners

Dr. Amna Mirza

Dr. Amna Mirza is an alumnus of prestigious educational institutions like Delhi Public School (Mathura Road), St. Stephens' College (Bachelors' Degree), Hindu College (Masters' Degree), United Business Institutes, Belgium, (Master of Business Administration), University of Delhi (Doctorate Degree).

She has been a meritorious student with first class grades throughout with several prestigious awards & scholarships like Vinod Dikshit Memorial Award, UFJ award, St. Stephen's College Centenary Medal, Karan Singh Medal, Prof. C.J. Chako prize and Godfrey-Philips & Meow radio station 'Golden Ovary Award'.

Her academic interests took her to University of Fribourg, (Switzerland), University of Duisburg Essen (Germany), amongst others. A voracious reader, a regular observer and writer of current affairs, an avid traveller, assistant professor, with research interests in International Political Economy, Globalization and Indian Politics. She is also the author of the book 'Global Times, Federal Concerns'.

Globalization and Voices from Indian Practitioners

Edited by
Dr. Amna Mirza

SHIPRA

₹ 550; US$ 27.50

ISBN: 978-81-7541-710-6

First Published in India in 2013

Globalization and Voices from Indian Practitioners

Published by:
SHIPRA PUBLICATIONS
H.O.: LG 18-19, Pankaj Central Market, Patparganj,
Delhi-110092, Tel: 91-11-2223 5152, 2223 6152
Br. Off.: 4617/18, Ansari Road, Darya Ganj,
New Delhi-110002, Tel: 9650028065, 9810522367
E-mail: info@shiprapublications.com
www.shiprapublications.com

Acknowledgements

Compiling the book was a Herculean task. With immense pleasure, I would like to thank the people who have it made easy.

Firstly and above all, Thanks Almighty!

I owe a debt of gratitude to all the contributing authors of the book. Without their involvement and inputs, the book would not have got to its present shape.

I feel lucky to have parents like Mr. Mirza Siddiq Ali and Mrs. Kausar Parveen, my siblings Amin and Tuba who have been a pillar of strength. A special word of thanks to Adv. Mohd. Hamdulla Sayeed and Ms. Rahmat Sayeed for their pertinent belief in my endeavours.

I am grateful to Avantika Maken Tanwar, Neha Kirpal, Rajesh Jha, Pranav Karol, Nitin Narain, Shahwar Khan, Deepshikha Rathore, Amrinder Sidhu for their help and good wishes always.

I am also thankful to my teachers—Dr. Rekha Saxena, Dr. Aslam Parvaiz, Sanjay Rao Ayde, Dr. Ash Narain Roy, K. K. Anand, Dr. Vijay Sharma, Sasmita Satpathy—who have been a constant source of guidance and support.

Dr. Amna Mirza

Contents

Introduction

The era of 1990s with the ceasing of the cold war was heralded as the end phase of history. No one knew that time might have thought that this prognosis and projection shall be discarded by the escalation and ascent of the forces that were there to make the world a place which was marked by an ever growing symbiotic relation of inter-reliance.

This process is often entitled as 'Globalization'. It is often exclaimed that it is a highly queried term for few (like me), which may be immensely opposed (like the followers of Marx and left brigade), and often commonly accepted by majority as the way of life.

There is lessening and contraction of time and distance, level of transmission, communication and exchange are much faster now. Though reams have been written in the academic literature about this phenomena, per se, analysing it from various approaches—liberal, Marxist, institutional—amongst others, yet something was missing—the layman was still oblivious to apprehend the compound nature of it. The purpose of the book is to present an interrogation to fill up the void where an attempt has been made to prod and explore how as to this has been generating new stories and discernments occurred in lives of practitioners—doyens and amateurs alike.

The impact of market is affecting lives of people, nations, companies, ecology. In this on-going aspect what we find that as we are getting inter-dependent, there is also an uncanny and disconcerting notion that the power of our sacred states is getting concentrated. However, the astounding and yet remarkable feature is that the state is here to stay and not just let it be a totally occupied terrain for the market forces.

If at one point there are strains and tensions in coping with the new or its adversary effects, there are also new prospects and occasions of growth. The writings that one shall see in the course of the book are presented with a view to respond and react to the intellectual earnestness to know where have we come from and where are we heading to.

The writings in the book are multifarious and assorted. In this manifold, spectre, one can sense an impulse to be cognizant of the changes unleashed by globalization, inclination to tamper with new factors and scheme out a blueprint for the future using past and present to tender succour and assistance for the times yet to come.

The selection of the disciplines which have witnessed globalization was cautiously done in order to present to the reader a comprehensive picture which was specific and precise, and at same time points to the general contours. There is no attempt made to generalize for all. The voices of the Indian practitioners present the global world to the audience from their experiences on the field and work place. So as things went rolling, it was indeed a roller coaster rise. Meticulously chalking down questionnaires, endless mails, interminable reminders via calls, short message service (SMSs), Black Berry Messenger (BBM), keeping the ray of optimism upheld amidst despair of missed deadlines amongst other were things that happened as time moved. There was no fixed routine in terms of working hours and what was remarkably surprising that an eerie sense of zest used to engulf suddenly within amidst all the unnerving moments. In this expedition towards bringing together all articles, what was paramount was the quest to know more in the finite outside and inside.

'Healthy citizens are the greatest asset any country can have', so said Winston Churchill. The book takes pride in presenting the same merriment as the contributors here are one of the finest brains and souls of our country in terms of their dedication, commitment and efficiency towards their work. The book presents more than a dozen articles depicting the chronicle of the collision of their respective work domain with globalization.

Ashok Tanwar narrates the saga of the intricacies of the political processes showing how politics is not just about five yearly elections. It has a larger facet to it with globalization casting an influence over its working. Politics has transformed itself with direct relations towards transparency, accountability and professionalism. Diffused with the idea of politics is that of administration. S.M. Khan takes the debate to the next level by pointing towards tasks that lie ahead for the permanent executive.

Change is the law of life. Away from this philosophical virtue, laws have certain institutional values being free from passion, rational, value-free and neutral. Simar Suri indicates that law exists for justice, where in the current era the mechanisms to tender justice, which have been in existence since centuries in the judicial system, are in need of reforms. Supreet Gill Sidhu further elaborates on challenges for legal education in the country primarily as they are operating at a crossroad—the time is pulsating—whereas the regulations to govern are still archaic.

The global world is about trade-offs and bargains. As the state shed its moral and social responsibility, non-governmental organizations (NGOs) came into picture. Though supranational structures on humanitarian lines, like the United Nations, have been in existence since long, yet the mammoth problems and grave neglect by the authorities in power, have given a good leverage to rise of NGOs today. Shilpa Sonal narrates this idea of shared obligation towards society and concerns of the survival and stability of this notion vis-à-vis the working units that cater to it.

Taking a glance from the by lanes of glorious Indian history, a splendid thought comes across from the teachings of the father of our nation Mahatma Gandhi who held that one has to learn in a manner as if one has to live forever. Education is important for national development and social capital of the nation by the virtue of its informative and awareness aspects. Seema Kaushal gives further understanding of the issues, that underlie within, by relating to factors like skill development, importance of co-relating things beyond classrooms, rural-urban divide and need for changes ahead.

Twentieth century is replete with instances where people have fought against totalitarianism and conservative tones. The twenty first century global era, with the free flow of goods and services, trade, finance, competition has proved to be a boon for the corporate business world. Sandeep Jajodia, here presents a fine distinct version of the inside story of a corporate office, wherein there are numerous challenges engulfing the organisation where consumers are vigilant and easy to change preferences. These, indeed, present new challenges on part of human resources and calls for pondering over avenues to translate then into opportunities.

The current times are perplexing, sorrows of the past and anticipation of future problems adds more than a little to our concern for well-being. Dr. Sujoy Shad takes the cue from this evergreen notion of 'health is wealth', and presents an argument as to how ironically the market forces are regulating former to a level, where latter has become its guiding principle.

As we move on, one cannot help but point towards the fact that current global times are fuelled by information where media has risen to become one of the most important entity. It is often said that whoever has the power over the screen can regulate the minds that watch it. Vedabhyas Kundu acknowledges this power of media and attempts to present an argument to make it work better by propagating media literacy.

If a picture is worth a thousand words, then Archana Bahl Sapra takes the arduous chore of putting her inkling on the canvass of contemporary Indian art scenario with respect to challenges and opportunities presented by the global terrain. Besides offering an intellectual preview of the world of creativity, the book has something for your taste-buds also! Food has been an important element of social culture and fundamental to life. Neeraj Tyagi makes us relish the flavours in the worldwide scenario, examining the changes in the industrial and macro-economic arrangements, changes in behavioural choices and illustrating an innovative setting on the Indian platters now.

Our lives have become a strange calculation and arrangements of things that are indigenous and those which we adapt from outside. Quite often, globalization is critiqued as 'aping the West'. Debunking this notion and putting forth a motion, Rachna Sharma argues that future of industries in India like hospitality lies with endeavours to opt for global best practices with a goal to embody it with our local needs keeping in mind issues like sustainable development. Abhimanyu Singh Arha focusses on the need to tap in benefits of globalization to usher benefits of culture, tourism and increasing the clout of magnificient locales of Rajasthan.

Everything has its pros and cons. Globalization is no different. The great growth and development that has been put forward may have certain fault points. There are also critiques who argue that idea of inter-change and exchange that globalization puts forward is nothing new. Trading and exchange relations existed even in the past as seen in the Silk Route.

With the failure of Keynesian model of economics, unbridled capitalism received a new impetus and free market forces dissuaded the idea of state intervention. Globalization brought along with itself the baggage of structural adjustments where the developing nations has to orient their economies and programmes as per the tunes of the developed ones.

With consolidation of capital in the hands of few, restrictions on the mobility of labour, technology there was action and mobilization from those who were displaced in this process. Cyriac Kodath gives a first person and real life experience of the movement. So as globalization weakens national boundaries and lures humankind with revenue and development yardstick, he gives an account of being a part of a movement where the fishing villages of Vizhinjam, Adimalathura and Poovar are being risked permanently in the name of supposed development. He narrates how the local forces have decided to caste a voice against uprooting by global dogmas.

So you embark on the journey to scan through the reams of the book, here's wishing you Happy Reading! The writings presented here are an approximation of reflection of current scenario. There is no claim made here that this is the final picture. The voices here shall strike an empathetic cord with all and here in lies the great utility of the book—that is to learn from each other's diversity, consolidate past gains and accelerate towards higher aims in future.

The various practitioners present the mirror image of the global world from an Indian working scenario prospective. There may be areas that the book may have missed or could have incorporated. The reader's reviews shall surely be the yardstick in this regard for my future work.

Ashok Tanwar

Ashok Tanwar is an Indian politician, Member of Parliament from Sirsa (Haryana) and Secretary, All India Congress Committee. He is also a former president of National Students Union of India & Indian Youth Congress wherein he has the credit of being the youngest person to occupy the post. He pursued his education at Jawaharlal Nehru University's centre for Historical studies and completed his M.A., M.Phil and Ph.D from there.

1

The New Indian Political Milieu

Ashok Tanwar

The article attempts to present the nuances in real time operation of politics in current times. The central argument made is that there may be problems and drawbacks, yet the silver lining in the cloud is that our politics based on democracy and working for people, has always been robust.

The significance attached to the realm of politics can be read from what Aristotle held as one of the 'master sciences'. It is something that pervades in other realms of life also. The nature of politics is clearly elaborated by its nomenclature from the Greek word 'polis' which meant the city state. It therefore connotes an activity towards the larger good of the society. This exercise gives meaning to our existence in terms of our rights, duties, liberty, and justice and therefore forms the core of any question.

As we begin the discourse, it is essential to know that Indian political system is unique in its own as its tries to factor in unity with all our diversity, it seeks to move along with rural and urban, it strives for empowerment for all, in a nutshell it is all inclusive with no discrimination towards any person based on caste, creed, region. The successful start of our parliamentary democracy can be seen from the fact that even after six decades of winning freedom, the various nations of the world look at India's experiment in universal adult franchise as a commendable instance of having faith in dignity of humankind.

The contours of our political system were given a marvellous start with the ideas of Nehru, Mahatma Gandhi and Maulana Azad. The impetus gained after winning the independence made the national struggle find its continuance with India largest party–Congress party. It was often called as an umbrella organization because of its inclusive nature where all segments of Indian society were represented. In the post independence era, India emerged as a federal republic with parliamentary features, where there is clear cut division of power between the centre and states. The states are heterogeneous and diverse owing to their geography, culture, society, etc.

Leaders like Nehru with their extra ordinary erudition and command amongst the realities of the ground built the foundations of our parliamentary democracy. He commanded power over the affairs of post independent India for twenty six glorious years and the basis for this were built on the high respect that he commanded as one of historical stature. As responsible president of the ruling party and the government, the party led the nation towards the arduous task of nation building against the backdrop of traumas of partition. With Nehru's personal charisma and the towering reach of the Congress party, India came to be known as a one-party dominant state because the Congress party always won general elections and the opposition was splintered. This was carried by Indira Gandhi and Rajiv Gandhi also.

The stability of political system saw its ups and downs in the post 1989 era which witnessed the government being carried by the coalition of parties. Today politics may be marred by different problems, yet the process is here to stay. Just like we may criticize Indian parliamentary democracy, but we have to take pride that it is one of world's most successful functioning system.

The history of the modern world can be briefly read as beginning with the First World War which was primarily pan-European, then the Second World War which engulfed the entire world powers, the cold war which made the world to be seen towards the bipolar lenses of capitalist versus the communist. In current times, geography is under re-configuration, that the social, cultural, economic space is no longer tracked with reference of territorial places and borders. The onus is on the new generation to look into how this phenomena shall affect the notion of politics.

The end of cold war marked the end of the era of looking at socialism as the only option. There was an effort to look at market along-with the planning by the state. A globalizing India has now to deal with international standards with need for international economic coordination much more than past. India has changed course and politics of today indeed justifies that.

The Thorns and the Roses

Huge expectations of people, our rising numbers, and limited supply of resources indeed present a complex picture in the system where only your performance has to be your yardstick for evaluation at periodic five year elections. Politics is a tough and meticulous duel of unlimited demands in terms of concerns of the electorate but limited supply looking at the resources to be able to deliver varied expectations. This journey is made even more rickety as it springs from the third tier of Panchayats to the central level, with the diversity of language, regions, customs and democratic elections.

Politics is often called as the art of impossible. Quite often the image of being close to corridors of power makes you vulnerable to peer pressures to misuse the same. The growth in politics is a gradual affair. It is does not happen all of a sudden. However, there is no room for surprise as the story is no different when looked at other work avenues like cinema, arts, sports, medicine, management that things happen with time. One has to carefully adapt oneself to the discipline and learn the rules of the game, and then take the larger plunge.

Growth and Development take place keeping in mind the needs of the time. It may require tough decisions yet that lays the solid groundwork for needs of future generation. Indira Gandhi did it in case of Bank Nationalization, Green Revolution, Rajiv Gandhi in case of Information Technology revolution,

Sonia Gandhi in case of Right to Information act, right to work, amongst others. The current UPA II regime by allowing 51 per cent FDI in retail sector and opening up other sagging sectors like broadcasting and aviation for foreign investment, efforts for food security bill indeed presents a great example that how politics needs to constantly re-invest, question and re-define itself keeping in mind new environments.

The need of the hour is to propagate the idea of inclusive growth, where political parties have to give voice to the people at the grassroots. Electrification of rural household, increase in tele-density, water supply and increase in irrigation have been pursued under country's rural infrastructure programme *Bharat Nirman,* which indeed tell the saga of the need to empower the grassroots.

Politics of today has to deal with various issues which are dynamic. Thus focus now has to be diverted towards balanced growth and need to strike equity in policy outlines. To assume that things shall change by a bing-bang approach is a chimera. It requires piecemeal change towards social engineering. The right based or entitlement approach is a unique concept in the growth and development plank which was a game changing positive transformation of power relations among the various stakeholders. By emphasis on right to information, employment, education and in near future food security, a great leap was taken to strengthen the capacity of duty bearers to empower the rights holders.

Therefore, the nation presents a different story now. India is one of the leading growing large economy in the world, where there is record food-grain stock, power generation capacity has increased, new highways, increase in foreign direct investment, nearly 100 million new phones, internet and broadband connections. the average life span of an Indian has gone up by five years in the last nine years of the Congress led-United Progressive Alliance. Further, number of people below the poverty line has gone down from 400 million in 2004 to 350 million in 2010-11. Consistent efforts have been made for development of all sections and regions together-with anti-poverty, minority development schemes, central government grants to states and union territories to the tune of Rs. 32,900 crores.[1]

The complicated nature of the political process was aptly underlined by Rahul Gandhi when he dubbed 'power' as 'poison' at the Jaipur *Chintan Shivir* in January 2013. He put forward a need to do away with centralization and filter in accountability in democratic structures. When we hear saga of meritorious not being able to make it to elite administrative jobs, the sordid judicial delays, marginalization experienced by women, minorities, amongst others portray a sordid picture. This calls for churning out new means of operationalization of politics so as to be related to a larger goal of achieving a united prosperous nation. The challenge for the generation of today in the country can be explained as our nation requires a system in which man's progress is based not on who he knows but on what he knows.[2]

Our country is a land of billions. The task for us is to relate our education to reality and tackle unemployment by factoring in skill development. It is high time that we urge reforms in this realm. Further, the future lies with the youth. An attempt has to be made to include them in the process of governance. The Congress party took a lead in this realm by launching the unique initiative of *Buniyaad* which was attended by delegates from all across the country to give young voices a platform to experience and nurture themselves in politics.[3] The process of nomination shall pave way for democratic elections. It is not the boss favouritism or bonhomie with seniors that can fetch one a place in the organization, but own interest, merit, strength and capacity. This process of free and fair elections is quite similar to that of the Election Commission of India.

'A week is a long time in Politics', as opined by Harold Wilson. This sayings of era of thirties is aptly justified today in twenty first century as we live in an age of information and technology. With the rise of 24×7 electronic media channels, politics is no longer a passive activity. It has made attempts to broad base its agenda keeping in mind the new concerns. Communications is integral to the economy and culture that quite often, we in term present times in as information age. Unfortunately, if media boom is saga of current times, then it has also shrivelled notions of civic and political engagement.

There is a serious crisis of content and quality in media reportings. Absence of ethics in reporting sparks doubt of credibility that it shall crunch the deliberating means in democracy. No doubt, technology has made an impact on lives of millions of Indians. The challenge for politics is how to take this momentum forward for translating out energy and efforts of people into positive engagement for the betterment of nation.

Further the aspect of succession of leaders from one generation to the other, within the same family *vis-à-vis* dynasty, may give a platform. The nuances of the current age have made politics agenda oriented work, whereas the survival in the long shall be contingent on your own performance instincts. It is one's tenacity to be able to deliver that shall add value to the family name, as the needs of the time demand work oriented approach. Further, one need not be complacent at any point of time. Being a public representative implies a dedicated duty which demands tremendous personal sacrifice.

India today is witnessing rise in corruption, that even most of the political parties are plagued with this disease. There can be no dispute on the urgent necessity of combating graft and corruption in public life. However, initiatives of surrounding the government with pressure tactics in form of hasty passing of legislation as seen in past fail to stand short of parliamentary supremacy and representational legitimacy.

The claim to legitimacy of the self-appointed civil society actors, who have a tendency often to blame the politician and systems for all the evils that plague our polity, is indeed thin. Today, there are multiple stake holders that have a decisive say in governance like media, corporate houses, vested interests of certain civil society groups and NGOs, universities, other private players. Delimiting the agenda of corruption to the institution of executive and legislature is a blinkered vision of current global reality.

In this notion of 'soft target', we never think that today governance exists under multiple layers. We need to expand this notion of accountability, which includes not only political representatives, but several others players in the public domain.

Terrorism, naxalism, regional disturbances, amongst others has been used as a political weapon by few vested interests to achieve the ends by creating the fear and panic. As Harold Laski once opined 'eternal vigilance is the price for liberty'. We need to prevent ourselves from giving in to such divisive forces and work together for a comprehensive movement to let the nation stand united amidst all moments of crisis.

Our political institutions are a system of rules and incentives, wherein they are endogenous—rules, designs, structures which are indeed a potential variable in the administrative and developmental processes.[4] There is an urgent need to sensitize the masses about respect for our political institutions. The Parliament of India is a supreme body as a deliberative forum which represents the issues of the people of India.

However, this idea of our law making body is put under a dark shadow when looked at the recent washout of the various sessions of Parliament. It is an undisputed fact that the nation needs transparency in governance with no toleration for wrong doings at the expense of welfare of masses. The government of the day alone cannot be a single factor to let the house run. The working of the democracy also requires a responsible opposition.

To demand accountability is obviously desirable, but if the demand comes at the cost of a hostility towards working of our democratic institution, it tantamounts to hurting the interest of Indian citizenry whom we represent and a depraved stand towards pending welfare legislations.

Our political milieu and interface with the representative is marked by absence of mature opposition which forces the nation to engage itself in a democratic exercise where participation and deliberation are the defining ethos. Sheer resort to holding the house to ransom by the opposition forces makes a mockery of our representative institutions.

Today everyday news is filled about pessimism of the people with the political process in context of assertion by the civil society. The new Indian political milieu has to make efforts to restore the faith of the common man in the political party system. Instead of giving whimsical arguments about doing away with political parties, we need to renovate and re-establish the conviction and reliance between the leaders and the governed that has always been our hallmark. Our political process has always been resilient amidst all odds. Politics in India has had glorious past, this past has to send a telling message to the future that apt work is being done to solve problems of today.

REFERENCES

1. Swaraj Thapa, 'UPA-2 anniversary today, report card to outline work done in the last 9 years, *Indian Express*, New Delhi, 22 May, 2013.
2. Speech of Shri Rahul Gandhi, 83rd Plenary Session, Rajiv Nagar, Burari, Delhi 19 December, 2010.
3. 'Rahul Gandhi inaugurates the Youth Congress Convention in Rohini', Pressbrief.in, New Delhi, 29 November, 2011
4. R. A. W. Rhodes, Sarah A. Binder, *The Oxford Handbook of Political Institution*, New York: Oxford University Press, 2008.

S.M. Khan

S.M. Khan is Director General of Doordarshan News, a senior Indian Information Service officer, 1982-batch Indian Information Service (IIS) officer, who was also with Central Bureau of Investigation (CBI) as its spokesperson and Press Secretary to then President A P J Abdul Kalam. He has done his M.Sc. (Economics) in Social Development Planning and Management from University of Wales (UK), and LL.M. from Aligarh Muslim University.

2

The Changing Face of Steel Framework

S. M. Khan

This article tries to present an understanding of nature, working and scope of Indian bureaucracy in the era of current globalization. Though there are claims being made on demise of state, yet it is imperative to comprehend that factoring-in of reforms, appreciating the complex nature of administrative work and also receptiveness to new changes shall go a long way to let the steel framework—i.e. our permanent executive inculcate accountability and transparency.

The bureaucracy is the non-political arm of the state which is responsible for managing its public affairs. The literal meaning of this term is rule by desks or offices, where the task of a bureaucrat in layman's language is to implement government policy. The idea of Bureaucracy can be linked to the German sociologist Max Weber who sees it as most ideal type of organization defined by rationality, anonymity, division of labour, separation of professional and private realms, hierarchy with unity of command, job specialization. There is emphasis on formalized rules to ensure efficiency and predictability. The interface of an individual with public administration is from the cradle to the grave, therefore it is indispensable.

Civilization and administration have always lived and progressed with each other. The oldest bureaucracy can be traced to ancient Susa in Iran. Ever since the dawn of human civilised living, bureaucracy has been seen as an organ of public administration to take charge of work on a massive scale. To take examples from history, the Persian Empire, Suez City states in Egypt owe a lot to the bureaucracy in terms of team of architects, engineers, who were responsible for major role in management of the control of the empires and kingdoms.[1]

Beginning with Woodrow Wilson, Public Administration and bureaucracy in America were seen as the 'government in action' which was supposed to govern independently from the elected branches of government. The end of Second World War made the study of administration towards quantitative analysis and operations research techniques, which can be used for decision-making and other studies. The Hawthorne experiments further demonstrated how organizations need to take into account the considerations of the social environmental forces. The post-colonial era witnessed immense rise and growth in terms of expertise, power and institutional capacities of the administration everywhere.

Development planning did lay down an elaborate scheme of national reconstruction and development in terms of several well-planned social programmes. However, lack of proper implementation, red-tapism, and procedural delays led to lack lustrous output as plans failed to achieve outcome.

The era of twentieth century saw massive growth of bureaucracy. The rise of welfare state in capitalist and socialist system led to enormous expansion of its functions. Simultaneously with rising expectations of the masses new pressures built up as a crusade against bureaucracy labelling as being callous towards people's needs.[2] The result was dismantling of the welfare state and rampant privatization which have further led to new crisis where there is a need to balance chaos and crisis.

The Indian Situation

Indian public administration with its steel framework of bureaucracy was shaped during colonial era. It is looked upon as an autonomous power centre which has the full protection from the Constitution and judiciary.

The aftermath of partition with traumas of bloodbath, destruction, loss of lives and separation of important areas made it imperative to work the aspect of nation building. The need to build up national infrastructure with limited resources was a hard-hitting work. This was made easier by the bureaucracy who worked with anonymity in its character and dedication towards the Constitution of the land as the permanent executive.

The Preamble to the Indian Constitution makes a ringing declaration about the nature of our state—'democratic, socialist, secular, sovereign, republic'. The Indian state has always been seen as a welfare state where the government is seen to exercise a decisive say in management of the forces of market, as distinct from *laissez faire* state. The welfare and prosperity of the society is contingent on the efficiency of the administrative arm of the state.

Administration has always been a stabilising force in society as governments may change from one regime to the other, but the permanent executive is here to stay. It gives a remarkable degree of continuity between the old and the new establishment.

The era of 1991 marked a different trajectory in Indian economy with the move being made towards the regime of integration with global forces and opening up various sectors of economy. With the impact of the New Economic Policy, bureaucratic apparatus also had to undergo changes. More adaptive attitude towards competition, deregulation of government controls, downsizing of departments, more space to private and non-government forces, reducing of state role in social sphere like health, education amongst others were the changes witnessed. The policies became more positive in terms of reduction of tariffs, relaxation of foreign exchange controls and allowing foreign capital to participate in the process of development. Shared economic sovereignty and decentralization, are hallmarks of federal market economy. Along with complexity and fragility of the multi-party coalition era of present times have sapped executive capacity of governments.[3]

Challenges of the Global Era

To begin the debate on globalization and bureaucracy, let us search for a concise definition of globalization. The process can be referred to increasing supra-national connections beyond national borders since 1970s, which was at its zenith in 1980-90s and today in twenty first century, which is here to stay.

Ease and rapidity in flow of goods and services, trade and competition have been its hallmarks. Therefore, the answer to the perplexing question as to what are its aftermaths and effects require an analytical approach where one needs to ponder over certain clauses like globalization has many dimensions, so has bureaucracy—namely social, economic, cultural. Globalization is an independent variable whereas its impact on the territorial systems has been dependent variables on the degree of operation of global forces.

With the role of the state undergoing a change in today's time, bureaucracy cannot be immune to the process. The task for the civil servants today is to work out things in a manner so that effect of global forces on the domestic land is factored in to the best possible level, in terms of minimising its harmful content and maximising the beneficial intent.

The erstwhile method of policy formulation was top-down, where the goals and objectives were fixed at the top level which were later passed on to down for implementation. This method of policy making has come under immense critique and thus subjected to change in the global era. Though even today policies are made under the golden rule of separation of politics and administration, yet there is a change in terms of mechanisms so that goals and policies are made under flexible module where the needs of the client are important. The grassroots are no more a passive recipient of policies from above, but have an active say in giving inputs.

In the realm of implementation of policies, today policy makers have to consider how they can expand their interests in realms beyond the national borders. The global forces have made it imperative for the state and government to make policies that enshrine increasing links between nations and their economies. While signing international agreements and other treaties, one has to factor in its ramifications and impacts on the grassroots. Climate change is an important example here where policy makers have a tough choice of trade-off between development at one hand and ecology on the other.

When we perceive of quick communications, better connectivity, faster people to people contact, one can draw an inference that today living in isolation is no longer an option. The era of globalization is changing world politics that even smaller nations can exercise their say in big international matters. International financial and trade institutions affect the domestic policies of a sovereign nation.

With localization of manufacturing and re-allocation of expenditure as per efficiency yardstick, supranational global forces seem to present a complex web of alienation between public and private sectors where instability has grown with decline of parallel social security nets. Market, in itself has an inherent deficiency of limited information which complicates matters more.

The global forces are here to stay from where they can be no looking back. Thus, the picture that comes out is globalization and bureaucracy is linked in a web of inter-dependency.

Globalization has its own pros and cons. If on one hand it has ushered in competition, it has also promoted unhealthy conflicts, if it has broadened the spectre of democracy, it also adds news burdens in terms of more accountability, public concerns now need to be balanced with that of markets, where a citizen is required to be much more vigilant in terms of one's rights and duties as a consumer. The imperative of the global time puts an onus on the administration to strike a balance between these odd forces.

The revolution in realm of information and technology has led to shrinking of space and time. This leads to more professional orientation in work culture and discipline of public administration on lines of the private ones.

The idea of citizen charter to ensure transparency in government, right to information, motivating the civil servants and above all promoting a stakeholder approach was propagated in 1991 in United Kingdom. Countries such as Belgium, France, Canada, Australia, Malaysia, Spain, Portugal, India etc. were influenced to adopt similar measures.[4] Today there are citizen charters that are placed at every government department. It is in nature of a statement of governments' commitments of quality service as an understanding between the two. The administration makes attempts to reach out to citizens, being in the veil of anonymity to broad base the inputs for policy decisions.

There is an attempt to reorganise the structures of the government in a simple manner and usher in more autonomy. This is seen as an attempt for achieving the desired results of productive performance and leadership.

Gone are the days when working in the government sector was seen less lucrative. Today's rewards and pay structures are getting linked to performance. The departments are undergoing changes in their cost and revenue management by switching from cash to accrual accounting, in an attempt to cut down expenditures and increase the surplus. The Sixth Pay Commission also recommended the introduction of performance based perks for Central Government employees for linking Compensation to Competence, which shall be separate from their regular salary.[5]

Governance is an illusive term with varied interpretations; to some it may mean process of selecting governments, while to others it may signify process of formulating policies with various stakeholders. Being a buzzword in today's lexicon, administration cannot remain aloof from its impact. The irony is that though we talk about socialism in our constitution, yet the reality of land, under impact of globalization—the divide between rich and poor in increasing—i.e. the rich are getting richer and poor are getting poorer. To add to that, massive corruption and unfortunate phenomena of criminalization of politics are hampering the good elements of the administration. The need of the hour is to work towards reforms to uproot these structural evils and cherish the tenet of governance to secure liberty, justice and equality to all with resourceful and competent policies.

New times have propelled old existing structures to work out new mechanisms of working. Today local issues have overlapping interfaces. They need to be worked by consultation and negotiation. Perhaps, realising it today that he have an era of e-governance in government departments, efforts are being made for computerization to use benefits of technology for education, health and taxation.

Due to large scale of computerization of services, reforms have been initiated due to which there is rise in awareness among the citizens. In areas like—hospitals, civil supplies, urban development, electricity and water supplies, e-governance has proved to be beneficial by eliminating middlemen and acting to curtail corruption.[6] Not only that, corporate players like Bharti, Reliance, TCS and Wipro are also joining this bandwagon by engaging themselves in preparing computer-based applications for delivering government services.

The article 19 of our constitution enshrines the concept of freedom of expression. The need to have information about how our Government and public institutions function and also to broad-base the idea of our democratic apparatus. We also have right to information act.[7] Democracy is a government as per the famous Abraham Lincoln idea 'as by the people, for the people and of the people', and this act places the very citizen at the heart and soul of governance.

Today we hear about the need to sensitize the citizenry to take up cudgels against the policy makers in case of any wrong doing by referring to the autonomous realm of civil society. There is no wrong in creating awareness about needs and concerns of the masses. However, this should not come at the expense of denunciation and condemnation of administration. The grim reality of present time is that one is self-sufficient and needs the other to fulfil the task. There is a need to develop concentrated efforts and collaboration between administration, market and civil society.

Though we talk about the global era, yet it is unfortunate that factors like Indirect tax costs, formal rules, restrictive regulations which are part and parcel of bureaucratic procedures have been responsible for trade barriers amongst nations, peoples and corporates.[8] Thus, it is important to work out modules to simplify procedures and ensure speedy work in administration.

In the past, there have been several committees which have voiced concern for reforms in Indian bureaucracy like Paul Appleby (1953), Kothari (1977), Satish Chandra (1989), Hota Committee (2004), namely legal protections to ensure that civil servants keep their integrity safeguarded, delinking politics and administration, employment of specialists and experts, new ways of recruitment, selection, rewards to be based on performance. A serious thought over these proposals shall go a long way to revamp the present system in tune with needs of the current times.

With all the gloomy arguments being presented after nearly more than a decade of liberalization about the future of the state, the reality is that the state sector is still one that caters to majority of the population. The 'steel frame' of the civil service has always been at the forefront to serve the rural India.

Though globalization is predicted as irreversible, yet there is serious scepticism about its efficacy, owing to the fact that its institutional basis is seen to be weak, and perceived losses seem to outweigh the projected gains. History has never been linear in social sciences. Further, international economic global governance is a chimera, with too many nations and differences amongst them. We have to choose between nation state and international integration, if we chose nation state then a nation has to deepen its role for democracy and deepen globalization.

Therefore, to conclude the idea of government is paving way for governance, which has a thick, concept of stake holders as the global has a connection with local and vice-versa. The bureaucratic apparatus has rightly sensed the mood of the present time where input base in decision making has been aggravated. Globalization may be working along to the benefits of few, wherein lies the challenge for administration, in a democratic apparatus which is to comprehend the complexities of the process, that the democratic institutions need to provide for impartial standpoint for equality of interests of all.

REFERENCES

1. Ali Farazmand, *Bureaucracy and Administration*, Florida, USA: Taylor and Francis, 2009, pp. 5-9
2. Maurizio Franzini and Felice R. Pizzuti, *Globalization, Institutions and Social Cohesion*, Hieldberg: Springer, 2010.
3. Lloyd I. Rudolph and Susanne Hoeber Rudolph, 'New Dimensions of Indian Democracy', in Lloyd I. Rudolph and Susanne Hoeber Rudolph, *Explaining Indian Democracy: A Fifty Year Perspective*: 1956-2006, vol. II, Oxford University Press, 2008, p. 322.
4. 'Citizen's Charter', www.sasanet.org
5. Aman Shrama, 'How to Fix The Five Problems that ail Indian Bureaucracy', *The Economic Times*, 2 May, 2013.
6. 'E-Governance Brings Down Corruption: Survey', Press Trust of India, New Delhi, 19 January, 2004.
7. Shailesh Gandhi, 'Right to Information—Path to Swaraj, *The Hindu*, 7 October, 2005.
8. 'Indirect Tax Cost, Bureaucracy Among Trade Barriers for MNCs: Ernst & Young Study', Press Trust of India, 9 June, 2013.

Simar Suri

Simar Suri is a practicing advocate at the Supreme Court of India. She has studied at premier educational institutions such as Carmel convent School, St. Stephens College and the London School of Economics and Political Science. She has represented India at the Japan East Asia Future Leaders Programme (JENESYS) on 'Comprehensive Peacebuilding Initiatives of Young Leaders in Asia and Oceania: the Potentials of Culture and Education'. Subsequently she was invited to represent India at the 'JENESYS New Beginnings' Programme held at Manila, Philippines. At present she is a senior associate at a leading law firm Suri and company, headquartered at New Delhi.

3

Globalization and the Legal Profession in India

Simar Suri

The legal profession is a service industry. It operates within the parameters set out in the Constitution of India read with the salient provisions of the Advocates Act, 1961. The ethical norms governing this profession are set out in the Bar Council of India Rules, 1975 and can also be found in several rulings of the Supreme Court, which is the highest Court of Appeal and in various High Courts.

India is governed by the rule of law, which rests on the three pillars of society: the legislature, the executive and the judiciary. These three organs operate within the jurisdiction carved out by the Constitution of India as interpreted by the Hon'ble Supreme Court.

What constitutes the rule of law and its implementation is determined and managed by judiciary on one hand, and legal professionals on the other hand. India follows an adversarial system of litigation. Advocates representing the opposing parties/ litigants assist the court to lay down the law and to spell out efficacious remedies.

Although the laws in India are derived from the common law system (e.g. laws as prevalent in England) as contradistinguished to civil law (e.g. laws as prevalent in Germany, Italy and France, etc.), it is pertinent to note that as of date, India has its own written constitution and is governed by statutory laws as enacted by the Parliament. Some of the areas in which laws have not yet been enacted, the judiciary has taken the initiative to lay down guidelines pending appropriate legislation by the Parliament. (e.g. the landmark judgment of *Vishakha vs. State of Rajasthan*[1] where the Hon'ble Supreme Court has laid down norms which ought to be followed by every organization, public or private, to protect women from sexual harassment at the workplace).

At the outset, it is pertinent to note that the right to practice law is a statutory right governed by the provisions of the Advocates Act, 1961 and the Bar Council of India Rules, 1975. Section 29 of the Advocates Act confers the right to practice the profession of law only on one recognized class of persons called Advocates as defined in Section 2 (1) (a) of the said Act. Therefore, a person is entitled to practice law pan-India if he/she has a law degree recognised by the Bar Council of India and has enrolled himself/herself in any of the State Bar Councils of India.

Traditionally, Advocates in India have rather been distinct from their counterparts in the United Kingdom even though the principles of law in India are based on the British Common law regime. Unlike the United Kingdom, Indian Advocates/Lawyers are not divided into two classes of legal professionals; i.e. Barristers who represent their Clients in Courts and Solicitors who advise their Clients on a myriad of matters affecting their legal rights, including advice on transactions etc. In India, these roles are merged and Advocates often wear both hats and advise Clients on corporate transactions while also advocating their causes before the Courts of Justice.

The number of persons qualifying as Advocates has been steadily increasing in India. Today, there are approximately 12 lakh individuals registered as advocates, around 950 law schools including prestigious National Law Schools, and approximately 4-5 lakh law students across the country. Every year, approximately 60,000–70,000 law graduates join the legal profession in India[2]. A majority of these Advocates represent Clients at the Supreme Court which is the highest Court of Appeal, the State High Courts, various District Courts and other judicial and quasi-judicial bodies. A large number of Advocates in India have traditionally either provided individual services, or have been a part of family operated law firms.

Conventionally, the legal sector in India has adopted a conservative stance with regard to its regulation. It has been built on an edifice of statutes such as the Advocates Act and the Bar Council Rules which prevent foreign lawyers from being granted access to the domestic legal market. In addition to creating barriers for foreign law firms to enter the Indian legal market, the laws governing the legal industry have also placed oppressive regulatory restrictions on Indian law firms. There are limits on the number of partners a law firm can have, advertising or soliciting business is heavily restricted, there are also strict restrictions on multi-disciplinary practice which prevents Advocates from entering into partnership with other professionals such as chartered accountants, tax consultants etc. to provide services.

These restrictions amount to the creation of a uneven playing field for Indian law firms, in contrast to foreign law firms which face no such restrictions in their home countries.

Moreover, in light of the liberalization of the domestic economy and its integral link to the world economy, there is intense pressure from the international legal community to liberalise the legal sector and facilitate free trade and services across borders thereby fusing the legal profession into a 'seamless transnational fraternity'[3]. However, it is imperative to consider the concept of globalization critically and introduce change in the Indian legal sector appropriately.

Changes in Legal Profession Domain

Over the last decade, a new trend is being noticed in the legal sector. In the wake of the liberalization of the Indian economy in 1991, which made India one of the fastest growing economies of the world, in contrast to the much maligned 'hindu rate of growth' (2%). The paradigm shift caused, in virtually every sector of the world economy by Globalization, has had a ripple effect on the market for legal services.

The changes observed in the Indian legal arena appear to have tremendous potential in addition to making the legal profession highly competitive in nature. Since the 1990's, a new class of Corporate Lawyers have emerged in India, primarily for the purpose of advising the domestic and commercial sector. This has also led to a spurt in the growth of law firms. These law firms have now developed vertical areas of practice in which Advocates specialise in the provision of transactional advice; advice relating to mergers and acquisitions, capital markets, securitization, project finance, intellectual property law, investment related laws and environment regulation. These conventional corporate legal activities came to the forefront only after economic reforms were enacted in India, exposing the country to global forces. The norms and practices followed by these law firms are reminiscent of those followed by foreign law firms based in developed nations such as the U.S.A. and the U.K.

This growing class of elite Corporate lawyers constitute the critical 'yeast' or the 'strategic who' of the legal profession and they are already at the helm of several crucial developments in the Indian legal sector. The growth of this lobby of entrepreneurial lawyers is likely to change the face of the legal profession in times to come. They already have the ability to influence several debates with regard to professional regulations, education at law schools, pro-bono and public interest projects, legal process outsourcing and new methods of legal practice, and new laws which need to be enacted to support economic reforms etc.

India has also seen an increase in the demand for 'in-house counsels' by the legal departments of several domestic and multinational companies to exclusively advise on their legal affairs.

Lastly, India is at the core of the Legal Process Outsourcing (hereinafter referred to as LPO) market. LPO's are popular as India follows the common law system and its people are fluent in the English language. Furthermore, the government also promotes the industry by giving LPO entrepreneurs financial incentives such as generous tax breaks and subsidies on commercial property.[4]

The Limited Liability Partnership Act, passed on December 31, 2008, is also seen by many as a precursor to the liberalization of the Indian legal sector. This Act provides businesses, including the professional services sectors and legal firms, with the decision making flexibility of a partnership and the limited liability of a corporation, coupled with low compliance costs. The one major breakthrough this Act has made is that of removing the cap on the number of partners in a law firm. Under the Indian Partnership Act of 1932, a law firm could have no more than 20 partners, beyond which it was deemed to be an 'unlawful assembly'. Members of LLP's also enjoy more autonomy under this structure with regard to the arrangement of their internal management. Partners are jointly and severally liable for business debts and internal organization is based on mutual consent. Lastly, limited partners only stand to lose their initial contributions and are not liable for the unauthorised and independent acts of their partners. However this model has yet not become a popular vehicle in India on certain tax issues.

The Indian economy is perceived to be competitive, but the perfect competition envisaged by economists is where there are a large number of producers and a large numbers of consumers who do not affect price. This situation does not exist at present in India. Most of the industries are operating as oligopolies and each action by one merits a reaction by another. Therefore, to overcome this situation, regulatory fora have come into existence, such as APTEL (Appellate Tribunal for Electricity), TDSAT (Telecom Disputes Settlement and Appellate Tribunal), AERA (Airports Economic Regulatory Authority), Anti-dumping etc. The latest in this category is the Green Tribunal where all environmental issues will be decided. International disputes are also being resolved through alternative dispute resolution mechanisms such as arbitration. Trade disputes etc. are also decided pursuant to GATT Agreements etc.

Under the Indian Constitution, treaties are respected and become a part of municipal law after endorsement and notification.

Arbitration has emerged as an important means of dispute settlement for businesses operating in India and foreign companies doing business with Indian firms. India enacted the Arbitration and Conciliation Act, 1996 on the basis of the United Nations Commission on International Trade Law (UNCITRAL) Model Law on International Commercial Arbitration.

All these changes are helping the flow of capital and goods across borders.

Therefore, although many developments in recent years signal the possibility of a liberalised legal sector, there is a wide chasm between the desire to integrate with the Global Community by the new entrepreneurial breed of lawyers, and the situation which exists in reality.

Foreign Law firms have shown an interest in entering the Indian Legal Sector since the process of economic liberalization began in 1991. The first three international law firms to enter the Indian market were Ashurst, White and Case and Chadbourne and Park. They were granted liason licenses for the purposes of information collection and dissemination. In 1995, Lawyers Collective, a public interest organization sued these law firms for exceeding the terms of their liason licenses and violating the provisions of the Advocates Act by providing legal consultancy services.[5] After fifteen years, the High Court of Mumbai ruled in favour of Lawyers Collective and held that these law firms were never entitled to licenses in the first place. These firms closed their offices in India and left, but the Indian market still continued to be an attractive market for international law firms. Foreign law firms circumvented the formal barriers for their entry by forging 'best friends' relationships with Indian law firms for the purpose of referrals, joint marketing and training relationships. Examples of such arrangements include examples such as Linklaters with Thawar Thakore & Associates, Allen & Overy with Trilegal, Clyde and Co's arrangement with ALMT legal etc. However, the recent dissolution of the relationship between Clifford Chance and AZB Partners points to the fact that these arrangements are often fragile and based on a shaky edifice of projected benefits which may or may not be realised. Foreign law firms yearn for a stronger foothold in the Indian Market.

In March 2010, the Madras High Court was presented with a case where a practising advocate, A.K. Balaji, filed a suit against 30 foreign law firms including big names in the global legal community such as such as Allen & Overy, Linklaters, Clifford Chance, Freshfields Bruckhaus Deringer, Integron etc.[6] Mr. Balaji alleged that these law firms/LPO's were acting ultra vires of the laws in operation in India by advising on corporate transactions and litigations.

In February 2012 this matter was decided by the Madras High Court. The Madras High Court allowed foreign lawyers to participate in international Arbitration Proceedings in India and advice clients on a 'fly-in fly out' basis as long as they do not practice law on Indian territory. This matter is sub-judice at the Supreme Court and its outcome remains to be seen.

The Idea of Globalization

Although there are many ways to describe the phenomenon of Globalization, in order to understand its impact in the legal context and weigh its advantages against its disadvantages, it would be useful to adopt the definition provided by the renowned economist and 2001 Nobel Prize winner Joseph E. Stigiltz in his book, *Globalization and its Discontents*. Stigiltz provides a halfway house definition between pro and anti globalization scholars and describes the phenomenon of Globalization as, 'the closer integration of the countries and peoples of the world, which has been brought about by the enormous reduction of costs of transportation and communication, and the breaking down of artificial barriers to the flow of goods, services, capital, knowledge, and people across borders'.

The integration of the economies of the world as we have witnessed in the last few decades would inevitably lead to a gradual globalization of the legal profession; for law is an applied science and shares a mutually symbiotic relationship with politics as well as economics. Globalization is certainly not an isolated process which focuses purely on economic activity or affects only a few people, rather it is a set of simultaneously occurring changes affecting various social processes and industries. The legal profession is just one of these sectors which cannot be protected from the influence of the processes of globalization.

Mihaela Papa and David B. Wilkins, both of Harvard Law School's Programme on the Legal Profession offer a useful and thought provoking analysis of the impact of globalization on the corporate legal sector in the world's emerging economies with a special focus on India.[7] Papa and Wilkins place the Indian legal profession within the matrix of the existing literature on Globalization and identify three strands of social processes identified by Globalization scholars in other areas to explain and analyse the present state of flux in the Legal sector in India. The three social processes employed by Papa and Wilkins are; economic globalization, globalization of knowledge and globalization of governance. The inextricably intertwined nature of these three processes as well as their ability to be analysed separately serves as a constructive tool to examine the current situation in the legal profession in India. In each of these three cases, Papa and Wilkins find that despite the conservative stance adopted by India thus far, with regard to the entry of foreign lawyers and law firms into the Indian legal fray, it is inevitable for global forces to affect and influence the legal profession in India.

Moreover, in light of the fact that India is a signatory to the GATS (General Agreement on Trade and Services) which is an organ of the WTO (World Trade Organization); there is a mounting pressure from external political forces for India to open up the professional service sector to member nations. The professional service sector includes the legal sector amongst a total of 11. At this point, India has only made specific commitments with regard to the engineering services.

As per Article I.2 (c) of the GATS[8], trade in services has been defined as the supply of service by a service supplier of one Member, through commercial presence in the territory of any other Member. The nature of GATS is popularly believed to be inclusive in nature and the expectation is that it will create an integrated global market in services. This, however, is only one side of the coin and even though GATS goes a long way in including developing nations in the global market, the primary fear or apprehension gives rise to emerging economies is that such an inclusion on a world forum would not be on equal terms.[9]

This coupled with the fact that the Indian Government has maintained a positive approach to free trade across borders makes it rather difficult to maintain a protective stance towards the legal profession.

India has moved forward in leaps and bounds since it opened up the economy in the early nineties in the aftermath of a foreign exchange crisis which led the country to default on loans. As a part of its new policy regime, which promoted a more liberal and market oriented economy, India took several important steps such as scrapping the industrial licensing regime, increased privatization, heralding of the Competition Act in 2002, reduction in tariff rates, etc. One would assume that it is just a matter of time before the legal sector is also formally liberalised in view of the economic reforms already in place.

However, a lot remains to be said about the reforms required to be implemented in order to liberalise the legal sector in light of the phenomenon of globalization.

The Advocates Act of 1961 regulates and consolidates the laws relating to legal practitioners in India, in addition to providing for the constitution of the Bar Council of India along with other State Bar Councils. The said Act imposes heavy restrictions, not only on foreign lawyers seeking to enter the Indian legal market, but domestic players as well. As per section 29, only Advocates are entitled to practice law in India. Section 24 of the Act prohibits anyone, other than an Indian citizen, from practicing law in the country, even if the foreign lawyer in question has a degree from an Indian Law School and confines his/her practice to matters which concern the municipal laws of their respective countries. Therefore, in theory, India still has a very restrictive policy as far as liberalization of the legal sector goes.

There is a quid pro quo relationship between global law firms which use corporate groups to aid them in expanding to the rapidly growing emerging markets while local firms strive to bring their infrastructure, norms and practices in conformity with global standards.

However, we must tread with caution as Globalization is not a new concept in India. Colonial India suffered heavily at the altar of Globalization at the time it was under the yoke of the British. Raw materials including the mineral wealth of India was taken abroad and finished products were brought to India. It created a huge trade surplus for developed countries and huge economic sufferance for the Indians besides annihilation of handicrafts and industry of India.

In principle, India has agreed to liberalization and globalization as evidenced from the GATT Agreements. But it is alarming to notice that imperialism creeps into the modus operandi of developed countries in one way or the other. For example, credits for carbon trade are based upon the basic premise that polluting industries of America and the Western World would continue polluting the world but all precautions and not to operate polluting industries would be the responsibility of underdeveloped countries. The fact that USA has refused to sign this treaty, ostensibly in their national interest, shows that globalization is a hammer to hit the underdeveloped world so that the concept works in favour of developed countries and against the interests of underdeveloped countries.

Therefore, Globalization is a word which is to be taken with a pinch of salt. This remedy is not a panacea for all situations. It has to be controlled and brought about after taking Indian interests into account. The present decision makers in India perform the role of trustees for future generations and are obligated to introduce globalization in such a manner and in such stages as suitable to India.

The Global World: Boon or Bane?

The merits of a Global economy can succinctly be expressed in one statement—'It has been said that arguing against globalization is like arguing against the laws of gravity.'—Kofi Annan.

This question is not as simple as is seems. *A priori* the idea of a global world is beneficial but the condition precedent is that it should truly be a global world and not the demarcated world of developed nations and underdeveloped countries.

Globalization in the context of the legal profession could be a positive tool of development, but it has to be critically appraised, and then appropriately introduced.

A Global legal fraternity would benefit law firms as well as clients in India. As the number of transnational deals is increasing, there is an opportunity for everyone to profit from the liberalization of the legal sector. The efficiency levels of lawyers increase in the face of stiff competition, the industry is likely to get more professionalised and Indian law students, clients and lawyers will get easier access to the expertise of foreign lawyers in specific professional verticals. Furthermore, liberalization also works to promote national legal expertise and retention of legal talent. Clients would have the benefit of exercising greater choice in the selection of law firms. There would also be an increased probability of negotiating a competitive price as a result of this increase in availability of good quality law firms.

Law can no longer be contained within national territories. There is a dynamic process of exchange and adaptation of legal systems which influence each other significantly. In the light of economic power shifting to Asia, India and China along with other emerging economies are likely to occupy a pivotal position in these changing times.

In light of this it is imperative to prepare ourselves for this wave of change which shall be brought about if the legal sector is globalized. As the Indian Finance Minister P. Chidambaram, correctly predicted in the first half of this decade; 'The failure to build legal capacity in matters concerning the economy is as grave as the failure to build capacity in our roads, railway, ports and airports. As India integrates itself with the global economy, the inadequacy of the legal system has become more glaring.'[10]

Globalization of the legal industry, if brought about in phases, will be a positive step towards the creation of a world without borders and will increase the opportunities available to

Indian law students, competition and will bring a measure of professionalis. Lastly, the boost to the GDP of the Nation accruing from the liberalization of the legal sector is definitely a positive factor to consider.

The Economic Angle, Global World and Law

The demand for legal services has witnessed a sharp increase in light of the spurt in economic growth. As per a prediction made by RSG Consulting; The top 100 Indian companies spent $479 million in legal fees in 2010. On an average, Indian clients spent $2.5 million on India-related legal work, while their foreign counterparts spent just over half as much at $1.3 million. India's Corporates giants, the Tata Group, Essar Group and Wipro top the list of corporate which spend a sizeable amount on legal services, paying out approximately $50m, $15m, and $12m respectively in legal fees per annum. Furthermore, a majority of top Indian corporations expect their legal spending to increase by as much as 11 per cent annually.

If the cost of in-house lawyers is added to legal spending, the total amount at stake in the Indian corporate legal market reaches well over $1bn annually.[11] There is a rise in the amount of cross-border transactions handled by Indian law firms and this has led to a greater demand for corporate lawyers.

India also occupies a dominant position in the LPO industry and the revenue earned from LPO's also add to the GDP of the country.

Indian law firms have also started setting up shop abroad to take advantage of the inflow and outflow of investments especially for venture capital and technology clients.

To meet this demand for skilled lawyers, even before liberalization, in the 1980's, the infrastructure was already put in place by the Indian Government to modernise and improve legal education thereby leading to a better equipped workforce in the legal industry. National Law Schools were established in the 1980's to train young students in the discipline of law along with a bachelor of arts, commerce or a bachelor of science degree.

They offer a comprehensive five-year degree discipline in law combined with a bachelor's degree. The quality of teaching at these schools is superior to that at other law schools in India for they focus on training law students for the profession instead of imparting merely theoretical knowledge. These students are trained to respond 'holistically and meaningfully' to contemporary challenges. The primary intent of these law schools was to improve the quality of the Bar. Ironically, however, it is noticed that a large number of law graduates prefer to join corporate law firms as opposed to LPO's, NGO's, the Civil Services, or even chamber practice under a Senior Advocate.

This sharp distinction between career choices in the post-liberalization area is influenced by several factors, however it seems as though the competitive salaries being offered by Corporate Law Firms or Multi Nationals as opposed to litigating lawyers or government services play a major role in moulding this choice.

The Bar Council of India alongwith with the Ministry of Law and Justice is ushering in reforms such as the creation of four regional 'centres of excellence', 'establishing an NLU in every State, creation of a new law library, an online e-learning network, more scholarships for disadvantaged sections of society etc.. The three year LLB Degrees are slowly being phased out to emphasise on quality as opposed to quantity of lawyers with a strong professional ethics. One significant move with regard to these reforms is the introduction of the All-India Bar Examination which is a mandatory requirement for new law graduates as of 2009. Other private law schools such as Amity Law School and Jindal Global Law School and the University of Energy and Petroleum Sciences in Dehradun are expanding their curriculum to include a multi-disciplinary analysis of legal problems and industry specific courses which equip students to enter the global legal community with panache. Some Foreign Universities may also be allowed to open their own campuses in India with the approval of the Bar Council.

Although these measures will lead to an increase in competition and quality of education, its real benefit to citizens of India will only be clear in times to come.

Therefore, it is clear that the Indian legal sector is slowly moving towards a culture that is seen in the developed nations currently which aims at providing legal manpower to the expanding corporate field. A new breed of entrepreneurial corporate lawyers who have a desire to emulate the professional practices of international law firms is on the rise. There is a global interchange of legal knowledge and traditions which adapt and transform in each jurisdiction to suit the needs of that specific jurisdiction. this globalization of knowledge has an intricate connection to the globalization of the economy as well as the globalization of governance in different jurisdictions. A change in any one of these necessarily affects the other two and vice versa.

Taking a cue from other jurisdictions of the world which have liberalised the legal sector for free trade, it will be wise for India to bring in progressive changes which encourage liberalization in a phased manner following the examples of South Korea and Japan. Japan adopted a cautious progressive approach in 1986 and completed the process of reforms only after 17 years in 2003. South Korea also opened its legal services market in three phases introduced over a period of five years. This cautious regulated approach to liberalising the market for legal services will give domestic firms a chance to fortify themselves and reduces the impact of a complete opening up.[12] It is important to be proactive while trying to achieve our vision.

The Way Out for Future

While liberalization of the market for legal services may be a positive development, it is important to test the waters in a phased manner to level the playing field between Foreign and Indian Law Firms in order to enable Indian firms to cope with the challenge.

Liberalising the Domestic Market is the first step. The Limited Liability Partnership Act, 2008, as discussed earlier brings in important changes, but does not specifically address the issue of law firm, liberalization. Restrictions on advertising should be removed so that law firms can solicit business just as their counterparts in developed countries. This also offers Clients the ability to make informed decisions. The Bar Council of India and the Ministry of Law must follow through on their suggestions for reform in the field of premier legal education. In addition to a uniform standard of legal education, successful lawyers must also be encouraged to disseminate knowledge to the rest of the legal fraternity.

Once we are on surer footing, we must allow foreign law firms restricted entry into the Indian Legal Market. It would be useful to do a patch test by letting them practice foreign law with clearly demarcated areas of practice at first. Joint Ventures should not be permitted at this stage to protect the domestic market.

Based on the reaction of the domestic players and the legal fraternity, the foreign firms could be allowed to enter into joint venture agreements and profit sharing arrangements.

Meanwhile Indian firms must look inward and strengthen themselves. They must merge their relative strengths and focus on gaining industry specific knowledge in different areas of practice.

Universities must also have an autonomous status and there should be a regulatory body for legal education. Law students should be made to focus on drafting and other soft skills. A centralised admission process is also beneficial.

Students should be trained separately for judicial services and legal practice based on their innate abilities.

As P. Chidambaram observed that a world class legal system is absolutely essential to support an economy that aims to be world class. India needs to take a hard look at its commercial laws and the system of dispensing justice in commercial matters. A beginning needs to be made at both ends. Creation of a Commercial Court Division within each High Court and the training of judges in the civil and criminal courts. There is no shame in admitting our inadequacies. Lawyers and Judges need training in economic and commercial matters. Likewise, economists and subject matter experts need training in legal principles. Together they will constitute the legal infrastructure that will have the capacity to deal with the myriad problems that arise in a growing and globalized economy.

The mutually symbiotic relationship between industry and legal services is only likely to strengthen over time. Industry shall get increasingly dependent on lawyers and the opposite will also hold true in this age of specialization and industry specific laws.

Mr. Rupinder Singh Suri, Senior Advocate sums it up rather succinctly that the metamorphosis in the legal services field is the awareness that a lawyer is a facilitator of an economic transaction and is not an obstruction. The laws, both national and international are so complicated that industry can no longer work as it used to do earlier i.e. act first and then seek legal advice. As of today, the industry has begun to realize that legal advice is required at all times from the beginning to the end, starting from the level of commercial communications itself. Each communication can help the industry in the generation or losing of revenue. Ten years hence, I envisage law firms with partners more than thousand or near about, having expertise to practice within the country and outside and travelling along with Indian multinationals to advice them and to negotiate with the laws of the industry of other countries developed or underdeveloped.

Conclusion

Historically, the study of the march of law has been in the context of dialectics as the law has been part of production relations, as contradistinguished to productive forces. Productive forces are unleashed by the dual interaction of man upon nature and nature upon man. The ever expanding productive forces demand an appropriate response from production relations for their efficacious operation. However production relations lag behind productive forces inevitably. As already stated law is part of production relations. In case production relations are flexible and dynamic and change is in consonance with the productive forces, economic growth is achieved exponentially and in the event that it is rigid and static, the situation leads to a violent change. It is in this context that the simple commodity economy transformed into a slave economy, the slave economy transformed itself into a feudal economy, the feudal economy transformed itself into a capitalist economy, etc.

To put it in simple words, if law is in accordance with the changing scenario of science, technology and production, the economy of the nation state will get a boost and if it is not, the law will act as an impediment to the growth of the country.

Therefore, there is a need to hone and shape law as per the changing needs of the society. (e.g. the Information Technology Act almost became obsolete by the time it was enacted because of extreme rapid economic changes).

The raison d'etre for Globalization is rapid economic growth of the economy and just distribution of the wealth amongst the citizens. This can only be achieved in case the right laws are enacted at the right time and at the right pace.

REFERENCES

1. Visakha and Others vs. State of Rajasthan, AIR 1997 SC 3011.
2. Vision Statement 2011-13, Bar Council of India http://www.barcouncilofindia.org.
3. Law and Globalization. 'Not entirely free, your honour'—*The Economist*, 29 July, 2010.
4. Krishnan, J. Outsourcing and the Globalising Legal Profession, William and Mary, *Law Review*, 48 (6), (2007). pp. 2189-2231.
5. Lawyers Collective vs. Bar Council of India and ors., W.P (C) No. 1526/1995 AIR (Bombay).
6. A.K. Balaji vs. Union of India, W.P (C) No. 5614/ 2010.
7. Globalization, Lawyers and India : Towards a theoretical Synthesis of Globalization Studies and the Sociology of the Legal Profession- Mihaela Papa and David B Wilkins.
9. Bibek Debroy, *Beyond The Uruguay Round: The Indian Perspective on GATT*, Response Books, New Delhi: 1996.
10. Law and Commerce: And the twain shall meet', the *Sunday Express*, OP-ED 7 Ahmedabad, 26 October, 2003.
11. 'Legal Eagles eye $ 479 m fee pie of India Inc." *The Times of India*. 17 March, 2010.
12. Liberalization of the Legal Market in South Korea; *Choi and Cho*, 2010.

Supreet Gill Sidhu

Supreet Gill Sidhu is an Assistant Professor at the University Institute of Legal Studies, Panjab University, Chandigarh. Her area of expertise is International Humanitarian Law, International Trade law, Private International Law, Intellectual Property Law and Women's Rights. An alumnae of Symbiosis Law School, Pune and London School of Economics and Political Science (LSE), London from where she secured her Bachelors in Law and Masters in Corporate Law respectively.

4

Redundant Laws, Dynamic Times

An Analysis of Globalization and its impact on the Indian Legal Education System

Supreet Gill Sidhu

> *"Law is today both a business and a profession. It deserves serious academic study so that students, consumers, policymakers and members of the profession themselves can better understand its role in our economy and society, and so that needed improvements can be made thoughtfully."*
>
> —Robert Joffe
> Presiding Partner of Cravath, Swaine & Moore LLP, USA.

The Indian legal profession is the second largest in the world, with more than 1500 legal practices nationwide and one million lawyers working as individual practitioners, in various types of firms and legal practices, as in-house counsels, as senior counsels, judges amongst others[1]. India alone has around one million lawyers, about the same absolute number as the US, although its per capita number is only a quarter or fifth of the US[2]. According to figures estimated in a report by the Ministry of Justice in the United Kingdom, the current estimated worth of the Indian legal industry is US$4 billion and is expected to grow to US$6.5 billion by 2016[3]. The Indian legal market is centered on the two economic powerhouses of Mumbai and New Delhi, with further legal and economic hubs to be found in big cities like Bangalore and, to a lesser extent, in Chennai, Kolkata and other cities such as Ahmedabad and Hyderabad[4].

The Past and the Present: An Evolution

The Indian legal industry has displayed a remarkable expansion over the years in spite of the ongoing global economic slowdown. The industry has slowly and steadily progressed and developed through self learning as well as drawing from experiences and development patterns of foreign legal industries. The structure of legal practice has altered by a long way in the last one decade and influences from the developed legal systems are most evident in the big cities wherein legal profession has seen a shift from Individual—Lawyer Offices to sizeable, more methodical Law Firms. Large city firms, which offer not only excellent legal knowledge and legal skills, but also good interpersonal and management skills have largely replaced the clichéd, behind the times lawyer, who was obsessed with legal precedents and nursed a blatant contempt for his client. In today's day and age, the key to become a successful attorney is not only being a good lawyer, but also being a good administrator who can skillfully provide satisfactory service to his clients alongside having excellent management skills. Advocates, in practice, are becoming increasingly aware of the importance of learning, developing and honing these skills. That is why law firms invest in an extensive internal training programmes, covering topics such as drafting and negotiating skills to leadership, supervision skills and networking skills[5].

The new breed of lawyers are fast shedding old-fashioned conservative ways of functioning and introduction of new teaching and training methods used in legal education at undergraduate and postgraduate level have an important part to play in it. Owing to the demands created by this new breed of lawyers, even the legal education system in India has witnessed a paradigm shift. The conventional three year law degree has been increasingly replaced by the more professional five year law degree which is both competitive to secure admission into and more rigorous to successfully complete. With the introduction of a handful of National Law Universities in the 1980's to the proposition that each State will have its own National Law School, legal education in India has come a long way and without a doubt that this is not the end, its just a initial phase which will revamp the entire legal education in India.

It was once said that students who fail to secure admission in the field of medicine, engineering or any other, are the one's who end up going to law school for the lack of choice. However, that is history now and gone are the times when law students were mocked across more competitive streams of education by belittling them with taunts like these. The field of legal education has undergone a phenomenal transformation and has come on par with various other sought after fields like medicine, engineering etc. A law school aspirant today, has to start preparing for his entrance level exams almost one year in advance, only then will he be ensured admission in the top National Law Universities of the country. However, the competition still is not over as one has to work hard throughout five years at law school and keep grades as well as extra curricular activities up to the mark in order to ensure a good placement with the ever so competitive law firms. A law student of today has no right to go on a holiday even in vacation time. Most legal institutions encourage their students to undergo legal and judicial internships with renowned law firms in various parts of the country so that they get an insight in the practical aspects of practicing law as a profession in addition to the theoretical knowledge they gain back in the classrooms. This contemporary drift is obviously an inevitable departure from the earlier legal education practices where law students got serious only during the times of examination. In the present cut-throat aggressive environment they have to be on their toes all the time where complacency and laid back attitude is just not acceptable.

Also, seeing an influx of students who register for these courses and later on the Bar, there has been a new development to keep a check on the quality and quantity of aspirants enrolling the Bar. Following the practice prevalent in the United States of America, a new Bar Exam has been introduced in India as well, where law students, after successful completion of their law degree, have to take an exam to gain admission in the prestigious Bar of Advocates.

Globalization: A Legal Academician's Perspective

In today's world of escalating intercontinental trade and interdependence of developed and developing economies on each other, there is a pressing need for a uniform transnational law which would not only provide a single system of governance but also would allow and facilitate legal practitioners and academicians to step smoothly beyond diverse legal boundaries.

The term 'globalization of law' can be understood to mean a certain extent to which an array of economies and their related practices stand to govern by a uniform set of legal obligations which may either be imposed and implemented by an international body, adopted by global consensus, or arrived at by parallel development in all parts of the globe. This process of globalization is evident in all facets of law[6] and the field of legal education is not immune to this change. There has been a remarkable increase in the number of law students displaying interest is studying and researching on subjects, which offer an insight into foreign legal systems ranging from the developed, developing to under-developed countries. Subjects like Intellectual Property Law, Cyber Laws, Public International Law, Private International Law, International Criminal and Humanitarian Law, International Trade Law, Space Law, etc. are just a few examples of new and upcoming subject which are rapidly replacing conventional subjects in Law Schools.

Opportunities and Challenges

Just like every thing in this world has a flip side to side, globalization too come has with multifarious implications on our legal education. On the one hand it has created numerous opportunities but at the same time, on other hand poses various challenges. Where on the one hand globalization has facilitated in intra-nation and interaction between judges, lawyers, academicians, practitioners and even law students, it has also brought us to a state of confusion with respect to established legal positions. For instance, in the field of Intellectual Property Law, or Private International Law, which is still at its conception stage in the Indian Legal System, in the event of confusion, decisions and judgments of foreign courts are cited for lack of judicial precedents in India. It is not only difficult but also dangerous to rely upon foreign law, both in the field of actual practice as well as teaching of law. For an academician, to predict the admissibility and validity of the stand taken by a foreign court, in the context of local needs can often be challenging and students sometimes are left in the lurch for a tangible solution.

Rapid expansion of information and communication technology has made it effortless to come within reach of foreign legal material as compared to few years ago when subscription to foreign judgments and materials were way too expensive to access. Now a days, the decisions of most constitutional courts are uploaded on freely accessible websites[7].

With the advent of globalization there has also come a massive intensification of Internet Protocol Networks, which in turn has led to immense growth in career opportunities of the law students. For instance, India has witnessed the phenomenon of the rise of Legal Process Outsourcing firms or LPO's which refers to the practice of a law firm or corporation obtaining legal support services from an outside law firm. The LPO provider can be based in another country the practice is called off shoring and involves the practice of out sourcing any activity except those where personal presence or contact is required e.g. appearances in court and face-to-face negotiations. When the LPO provider is based in the same country the practice of outsourcing includes agency work and other services requiring a physical presence such as court appearances. The most commonly offered services have been agency work, document review, legal research and writing, drafting of pleadings and briefs, and patent services[8]. However, the backlash of this is that some of the brilliant brains in law schools who should ideally be joining litigation or similar services are ditching all the hard work and taking a short cut to make quick and easy money.

Globalization has changed the whole political and social scenario of the world and as it has created multiple opportunities, at the same time it also presents many challenges before the legal education system in India. One such problem is the entry of foreign lawyers into India, which brings a tough competition, not only from within but also from outside the country. Though there has been a stiff resistance from lawyers and law firms opposing this change however, the ground reality is very different. Foreign law firms began showing interest in expanding to India in the early 1990s shortly after liberalization and a few also succeeded in setting up their offices in India for liaison reasons, such as information gathering and dissemination. However, in 1995, a lawsuit was brought against these firms in the Bombay High Court, claiming that the firms exceeded the terms of their licenses and provided consultancy legal services through their offices. The lawsuit alleged that the presence of foreign lawyers in India was a violation of domestic law[9] and after a lapse of almost 15 years; the Bombay High Court ruled that the original grant of licenses to the foreign firms had been done in violation Indian law and as a result of the ruling, all the firms were directed to close their liaison offices.

Also, the legal education in India is not equipped to confront new challenges and dimensions of globalization because of lack of uniform standards of curricula and syllabi, lack of expert faculty, insufficient funds, limited focus on teaching and research, lack of global interactions and collaborations and most importantly lack of recognition of foreign degrees. After a lot of hue and cry, the Bar Council of India, which is the governing body for recognition of Bachelors Degree in Law, finally published a list of foreign universities whose degrees were declared as valid for the purpose of practicing in India. However, with regard to Masters Degree in Law, both the Association of Indian Universities (AIU) and the Bar Council of India (BCI) seemed to have washed their hands off from undertaking the responsibility to give recognition to Masters in Law degrees obtained abroad. This has led to a lot of confusion as to who actually is the related governing body. Despite the fact that in January 2013 University Grant Commission (UGC), came out with the official notification stating that one year Master of Law Legislation (LLM) is to be introduced in Indian Law Schools and that both, one year and two year Master of Law Legislation (LLM) shall stand valid[10], there still persists an uncertainty on the future of Indian students who have secured their LLM degrees from reputed foreign universities. The University Grant Commission-National Eligibility Test (UGC-NET) office has been conveniently sitting on the certificates of such candidates despite their having successfully cleared the exam.

The legal education institutions, persistently, confront the challenge of sustaining international standards to convey quality education, lifting academic standards, infrastructure, devising good governance models, creating better career opportunities and upholding professional advancement[11].

The Future

Legal Education has traditionally been a neglected area in India where there has not been any fundamental change during the last 150 years, except for the duration of the courses and addition of some fundamental subjects[12]. If the law schools across the world are changing and evolving to cater to the needs of a global market, Indian law schools cannot conveniently choose to remain aloof from the inevitable. Indian legal education has a multitude of issues that prevents it from globalising its content—horde of regulations, class structures in legal education sector, and the problems ranging from inappropriate work load to dismal attendance in classes.

However, India, which is an emerging economy, has to soon tide over these issues and produce a uniform class of legal professionals suited for global competition. Half a century ago, the main purpose of university legal education in India was not the teaching of law as a branch of learning and as a science but simply to impart to students a knowledge of the black letter law, that is, certain principles and provisions of law to enable them to enter the legal practice exclusively for local needs. Gradually this perception changed and the process of reform in law and legal education was initiated. The real break came in 1990s when the new challenges posed by scientific and technological revolution and greater interaction between nations, trade in goods and services, information technology and free capital flow across international boundaries made the world a global village. Consequently, the concept of "local practice" widened to that of "transnational practice" in the context of globalization and opening up of most of the economies of the world[13].

Justice A.M. Ahmadi had said, ".... We have waited long enough to repair the cracks in the legal education system of this country and it is high time that we rise from arm-chairs and start the repair work in right earnest". The Law Commission in its 184th Report, (2002) has pointed out that there are revolutionary changes which have come into legal education by reason of developments in information, communication, transport technologies, intellectual property, corporate law, cyber law, human rights, ADR, international business, comparative taxation laws, space laws, environmental laws etc. and that "The very nature of law, legal institutions and law practice are in the midst of a paradigm shift." Globalization does not merely mean addition or inclusion of new subjects in the curriculum as stated above. While that is, no doubt, an important matter, the broader issue is to prepare the legal profession to handle the challenges of globalization[14].

Prof. David E Van Zandt of North West University School of Law in his article 'Globalization strategies for Legal Education' says that in terms of legal services, the changes have developed a standard set of practices that lawyers use in dealing with the needs of significant business clients whose operations have international scope. Whether a lawyer is working for multinational clients in Hong Kong, Frankfurt, London, Buenos Aires, or New York, the set of practices is largely the same. This enables a skilled lawyer to move effortlessly around the world.

The pursuit of better legal education and social awareness is now fueling another wave of reform efforts in this area spearheaded by the Ministry of Law and Justice and the Bar Council. The reform effort, as explained by the then Law Minister, Dr. Veerappa Moily, rests on three pillars: 'expansion, inclusion and excellence[15].'

In addition, the Indian government has promised to create a national law library and an online legal e-learning network, to increase scholarships and fellowships for potential students in disadvantaged sections of society. It also aims to focus on attracting quality faculty through better service conditions and remuneration and establishing a global standard research tradition. In proposing these reforms, the government aims not only to create and nurture a pool of talent, but also to focus on social responsibility and a strong professional ethic[16].

The Road Ahead

It is rightly said that legal education is an investment, which, if wisely made, will produce most beneficial results for the nation and accelerate the pace of development[17]. The legal education granted at the law schools should be aligned to the conventional and contemporary needs of the legal profession. Prof. C Raj Kumar, founding Dean of Jindal Global Law School has wisely opined that globalization has posed multiple challenges to the future of legal education in India, but it has provided an opportunity to challenge the status quo, which is an essential condition for seeking any reform.

In context of the above opinion, the education that is imparted to our future lawyers and judges in legal institutions calls for a serious and meticulous re-evaluation in order to bring them at par with the social and economic transformation that is underway in our system.

REFERENCES

1. "A perfect 10: what rates in the booming Indian legal market", Bithika Anand. http://www.lawcouncil.asn.au
2. http://www.lawyersweekly.ca
3. *supra*
4. http://www.legal500.com
5. "Legal Process Outsourcing in India". Hemant Batra. http://www.indialawjournal.com
6. "The Impact of Globalization in Legal Education in India", T.M. Devadas. http://www.answeringlaw.com
7. "Globalization and Legal education in India", Ashwani Tanwar. http://www.ssmrae.com
8. http://en.wikipedia.org
9. Lawyers Collective v. Bar Council of India and Others, W.P. No. 1526, 1995 AIR (Bombay); see discussion in Krishnan 2010 and Vena 2011.
10. http://www.ugc.ac
11. *supra*
12. "Global Legal Education and India—A Blueprint for Raising Indian Legal Education to Global Standards", John Varghese. http://papers.ssrn.com
13. *supra*
14. "Legal Education: Impact of Globalization on Legal Education In India", Sumit Kumar. http://www.legalservicesindia.com
15. Education Diary, 2 May, 2010.
16. "Globalization, Lawyers, and India: Toward a Theoretical Synthesis of Globalization Studies and the Sociology of the Legal Profession", Mihaela Papa and David B. Wilkins. http://www.law.harvard.edu
17. *supra*

Shilpa Sonal

Shilpa Sonal is a seasoned marketing & advertising professional and a social worker with over twenty years of work experience. In the recent years, Shilpa heads the 'Sanshil Foundation' where she has been actively involved in charitable and social work aimed towards uplift of the underprivileged children and vocational livelihood activities for adults. She has pioneered the model where green energy and ecologically sustainable practices are a source of livelihood for the economically weaker sections. Her main focus is on creating literacy programs and vocational training, with a new perspective, for children and adults from those at the bottom of the pyramid. Shilpa is also Secretary—SPIC MACAY Gurgaon—a Voluntary organization that is dedicated to promotion of Indian Art, Music and Culture amongst the youth. She is post graduate in Mass Communications & Public Relations (PR) from the Indian Institute of Mass Communication (IIMC).

5

The No-Profit World in Market Times

Shilpa Sonal

The paper attempts to understand the working of NGOs by first situating the debate on the context and situational aspects which have led to their emergence. The arguments in the second part of the essay revolve around the problem, issues, challenges and opportunities that the non-profit sector[1] has in the global era.

In a democracy like ours, NGOs have become an interface between the state and society. They have become harbinger of new hopes where their main role is seen as a catalyst to make the development process inclusive by making the gains of growth reach out to places where the state and government failed to make an impact. The registration of NGOs in India is covered under the Societies Registration Act, 1860 which is a central act. Our country can bask in the glory that not only it is an example of a great functioning democracy, but that it is also home to world's largest number of non-government, not-for-profit organizations.[2]

As per the UN standards, an NGO as a non-profit entity whose activities are determined by the collective will of its members in response to the needs of the members of one or more communities with which the NGO cooperates. It should be noted that private voluntary organizations, civil society organizations, and the independent sectors are often co-used with the word NGO.[3] The term civil society is a highly contested term in political lexicon signifying a realm independent and autonomous of the state. It signifies aggregation of individuals and organizations like NGOs as a sub-set within its larger structure. Women, children and youth, indigenous peoples and communities, non-governmental organizations, farmer's workers and trade unions, the scientific and technological community, amongst others are included in realm of civil society.

Today NGOs are seen to play diverse roles like mobilization of public opinion, giving space to the marginalized segments of society, providing technical and other forms of service (especially in health sector), giving a certain degree of legitimacy to state and international law policies, providing information beyond the bureaucratic set up, monitoring, assessment and government compliance.

Globalization—the process signifying increasing interdependence amongst the governments, people, companies signified by rise in activities of international trade, finance, investment, movement of capital, innovation, technology. The assimilation and amalgamation in this process has further effects on the environment, culture, polity, economy and human resources.

The development policy model after the Second World War period gave primacy to Keynesian ideas which gave important role to central government in regulating monetary structures. However, stagflation in 1970s, abolition of exchange controls has led to free market models of laissez faire being reworked upon in the Reagan and Thatcher era. The era of 1980 had a different tenor, and with the end of the cold war, where the faith reposed upon government intervention was shaking. The global market and its operations impinged upon the domestic apparatus which contested the power of the state. With the rollback of the state in every important sector like health, education, growth at the cost of environment, democracy was then just not limited to a political apparatus but expanded its contours in the form of a vigilant polity where avenues like new social movements NGOs came up.

Rise of NGOs has led to new changes in global economic and political scenario. The state cannot have a monopoly today in exercising the powers of information dissemination and of delivering results. There are new stake holders like NGOs that have come forward in areas. Further, what is essential to note is that they have even challenged the working of international organizations like the World Bank, the IMF, the UN agencies or the WTO in areas where there working and policies were remote from the realities of the grassroots. It has even produced greater opportunities for international business to tap in. Every policy maker and corporate agency is realizing the need for a dialogue so as to engage in the policies and matters of the society at large on a deeper level.

Thus the picture that emerges is what has been called as 'Governance'. Since the era of 1980s, governance has been a ubiquitous term. It is different from the term 'government' as it implies lesser focus on the state, wherein the process of governing is not marked by hierarchy. Market has its own in built process to develop rules. Thus, the scenario is hybrid, multi-jurisdictional and plural in its tenor. Current realm of governance combines people from different sectors and increasing diverse demands of stakeholders. The state is then found to be increasingly dependent on NGOs as its powers are constrained by the international markets and vagaries of global forces.[4]

As the market forces stabilized their role, the new actors in governance paradigm have demanded a more participative approach on part of the state in formulation and execution of policies. In the erstwhile era, the direction of power flow was in a top down manner, the realm now is much more broadened, decentralised and differentiated. There are new claims made for accountability and transparency by the non-state actors which have to a larger extent diluted the powers of the state. Thus, the traditional structures of power, authority and government have been weakened by the process of globalization.

Demographics and Psychographics play a pivotal role in defining the micro areas of a non-profit functioning. Unlike businesses, non-profits start with their mission and worry about performances and delivery. Today we have NGOs in various realms like education, health, environment social justice. Once established, then social intelligence, networking, marketing of products and right spread of awareness about initiatives undertaken for fund raisers and strategy mark the hemline of any successful non-profit today. Thus, the working and structure of a good established organization is quite similar to that of a business set up. However, what differentiates them is the goal-selfless devotion to the aim- and in some cases it may be upliftment of disadvantaged section of society, whereas in others it may be preservation of ecology. Once this mission is set up, policy advocacy is extremely important of the former with the government sector.

Today NGOs have specialized advocacy campaigning and fund raising departments. These openings in the social sector have opened up various opportunities indeed for the seeker and critique alike. It is held that unless one reaches out to the community for whom the goods and services are, one can meant do right business. There are various examples where corporate organizations are exploring avenues to work creatively and built up collaboration with NGOs.

Businesses can learn from non-profits today. Some of the management leaders of the day are turning to non-profits and making them more 'corporate'. And why not? Businesses would first worry about how much money went in and the returns. Employees in non-profit are driven to perform alongside with a strongly committed and self-motivated volunteer base. This rubs off on the success of the mission and results come flying by.

More non-profit are groups able to converge the management and employees of businesses towards community building and are long term 'charity partners' in growth. There is a focused view on social initiatives and not one time donations served across the table. Various verticals and top ranking CEO's have a clear view of CSR (Corporate Social Responsibility) policies drawn out and deliverables to the beneficiaries measured in terms of community work that is rewarded and recognized by the management. Further, this enables many businesses to also perform better by capitalising on their strengths and resources. Consumers also support the products from organizations which are socially responsible. One can add here the famous dictum that 'doing well is good for businesses', which catches the essence of people's interest in a corporate's attention to social causes.

Global firms continuously engage their employees on CSR programmes that strike a corner of their hearts for a social cause. This could be the most humane way to make businesses less business-like and more human. Non-profits are not about cut throat competition, even though money is never enough. Self-sustainability is a perpetual challenge and plans with not enough money can go completely awry. Non-profits have benefited tremendously in a more global world that we have today.

Volunteerism or as they say *Nishkaam Seva* works a like magical wand. It sees no language, caste creed or barrier except the mission ahead. Take the successful example of SPIC MACAY (Society for Promotion of Indian Art Classical Music and Culture amongst Youth established in 1977)—an organization that functions entirely on volunteers across the globe. Over 3,000 events are coordinated by students annually from Harvard, Stanford, Indian Institute of Technology (IITs) and Indian Institute of Management (IIMs) to the government schools in the remotest towns of India—all in the spirit of volunteerism and none of the co-coordinators worldwide are paid for any contribution they make. Orientations, District Chapter Development, Volunteer development and strategic planning, institutional cells, networking and reviving alumni cells are ways to route in volunteer induction.[5]

The idea of doing things without expectation makes one have the confidence and ability to connect with inner soul, which helps to attain a state of tranquillity and equanimity. Exactly what businesses can learn from what each volunteer performs because he is motivated to take the mission forward. And the time, energy and money he spends are not the take away he is looking for in today's fast food world.

The state sector in facing the challenge of reducing development expenditure and paving way for liberalization and privatization. As a result of aggressive competition, businesses are running on cost cutting models with ambitious desires to become Multi-National Companies (MNCs) and MNCs to be more global than they have been. The society is witnessing schisms based on this unequal distribution of resources in context of rising population, unlimited demands and limited supply that the rich are getting richer and the poor are becoming poorer.

An image of an urban set up has lightened up malls, mushrooming posh societies, avenues for recreation. Ironically, the latent: the slums with poverty, disease, malnutrition, lack of education; is never highlighted. The gloomy picture that emerges is that globalization and growth has tilted the balance of society in a lopsided manner. Whilst, we grow on paper and boast of growth, the hard realities of the Indian common man are far away from what the global common man is.

Yet, a global world means 'good news' for non-profits. Charities are talked about on social media, word spread is easier and fund raising more disciplined and organized. Going global feeds charities on big donations and CSR policies are common for a single business across the global. This increases the sense of belonging, identification of cultures, values, beliefs and social sensitization to the maximum output. Possibilities have increased manifold—rural products have found global markets and non-profits are able to take them across the globe. Visibility rides on the back of globalization and most interestingly, even the smallest employee of a large global firm will identify with the CSR.

In times to come, non-profits will exist manifold and businesses will turn to perform more like them in essence and spirit. Sensitization will usurp competitiveness and the mission will be the lifeline. Change must come and will. How else can growth sustain itself without collaborating with social issues and dealing with them? Disparity will only add fuel to the fire of crime and frustrations built on expectations to fulfil basic needs. Non-profits can successfully bridge the divide and make the global world come closer and close knit, too.

Non-profits will continue to impact this global world regardless of what a government can do. Every drop in the ocean counts, the life of every human being and animal can be touched and impacted, health services improved, a rag picker can be turned into an accountant and a rickshaw puller's son can dream of becoming a pilot. Non-profits are dream merchants of sorts and can contribute to change that society must come to.

Easy norms, fund availability and collaborations are the most important, factor in deciding the future of non-profits in India. Further, there is an issue of multiplicity of efforts which may lead to duplication of work being done. As per figures made available from government sources, it is held that ₹ 31,900 crore was received by over 68,000 NGOs operating in different parts of the country during 2008-11.[6] However looking at gigantic size of the nation, impact of NGO within a limited region, the arduous task of working for non profit enterprise in present competitive realm, these figures do not stand up to qualitative justifications.

Morality and ethics play a big role in credibility of an organization. The non-profit sector is also no exception, where doubt over working of dubious players put a question mark on the work and enterprise of others. Registration of thousands of NGOs was cancelled under Foreign Contribution (Regulation) Act, 2010 for violation of guidelines and many of them were referred to CBI for investigation. It is high time that we make efforts that heinous acts of few should not be made representative aspect for others who are genuinely doing good work. There is a need for carving out mutually beneficial approach amongst the state, market and non-profit sector based on transparency and accountability.

Today NGOs have made an impact on almost every sector of society. However when we see at an institutional level, there are no formal mechanisms for NGO participation within arenas like the UN system. Usually, when a summit or high level delegation is going on, groups of protestors on ad-hoc basis voice the concerns. The need of the hour is to develop mechanism to strengthen them into more organized forums and have an inclusive approach to issues by incorporating their concerns. Further, lack of mass media interest in NGOs owing to less monetary benefits in the era of 'PR' culture has led to lack of collaboration between the two. The practitioners from these two realms should encourage partnerships to enable the media to portray the real picture of problems of society which shall lead to institutional development among NGOs

Our country faces the biggest challenge in making an algorithmic change. Private public partnerships (PPP) for non-profits is the only way to cross the threshold of red tape and beaurocratic dismissals. The non-profit in the current times is business-like in approach—professional, disciplined, strategic, focused and armed with management techniques that require for it to be a successful venture. It follows the law of the land which makes it the best bet to rest a social cause on. A PPP can make it viable with infrastructure support and government clearances to reach the target audience.

REFERENCES

1. The words NGOs and non-profit have been used interchangeably at various places as they signify same meanings.
2. Archna Shukla, 'First official estimate: An NGO for every 400 people in India', *Indian Express*, New Delhi, 7 July 2010.
3. P.J. Simmons, 'Learning to Live with NGOs', *Foreign Policy*, Fall, 1998, pp. 82-83.
4. For further discussion see, Mark Bevir, *Governance: A Very Short Introduction*, Oxford University Press, Oxford, 2012.
5. http://spicmacay.com
6. 'Rs 31,900 cr received by Indian NGOs in 2008-11', Press Trust of India, New Delhi, 6 March 2013.

Seema Kaushal

Seema Kaushal is the Principal of the Ardee School Gurgaon. A post graduate in Zoology from University of Delhi, she has a rich teaching and administrative experience of twenty five years. As the head of the only Elementary Montessori school in North India, she has successfully enriched the Central Board of Secondary Education (CBSE) curriculum with the hands on and multiple intelligence elements of Montessori methodology.

6

Innovative Learning Towards Skills

Seema Kaushal

Education via its arduous ways of examination and emphasis on grades and marks has been seen as a yardstick for gaining acceptability in the world today, for various reasons from social recognition as being qualified to acceptability in the labour market. Education has always been linked to the idea of progress, at the micro level to that of individual, at the macro level to that of the society and nation at large.[1] However, in this link there is an important system of educational institutions, which have become important as we relate globalization and education.

Education is important in democracy to cultivate ethos like tolerance and rationality, respect of diversity, quest for stability, amongst others. The educational sector is one of the most indispensable elements of any economy. From times when good schooling was a privilege of a few to the current scenario where 'Sarva Shiksha Abhiyaan' and the Right to Education are upholding universal education till eighth standard for all Indian children, this industry is witnessing a huge flux.

The Indian scenario has witnessed a metamorphosis to Double Income Nuclear Families and largely single/double child household. This, along with intense global exposure has magnified the attention to detail on every step and has hence enhanced the need for better education. Also, the acceptance, that education is the means of transforming the quality of life has resulted in the demand for more schools. As a result, we are witnessing the mushrooming of schools of various genres—play schools, primary schools, higher secondary and senior secondary school catering to various pockets, different sensibilities and numerous permutations of teaching techniques.

The crux of globalization is the melting of boundaries and the barriers that hold nations apart. It is the international integration of people who share, collaborate and communicate to create a world citizenship based on personal and social responsibilities. Globalization has seen growth, both directly and indirectly in many sectors. Education is one such sector that has massively grown by passively globalized co-sectors.

The dissolving of cultural boundaries and narrowing of class divide through greater reach of education and technology that will result in the economic reconstruction of countries and is foreseen as the outcome of this phenomenon.

It is already visible in the country where Direct Investment has been seen not only in the Single and Multi-brand retail sector, but also Indirect and Semi-Direct Investment in the educational sector supported by efforts of the Government by encouraging international schools to mushroom and the implementation of the four-year graduation programme. Globalization is expected to contribute exponentially to not only our economy but will help Indian educational organizations to spread their wings internationally.

The other means, whose end is an open education sector, are accessibility, standardization and the growth of global citizenship that not only seeks but has sought to build international curricula and world-class schools. The International Baccalaureate in education has led to awareness about global issues, where critical thinking and pluralistic thinking take the focus of learning away from any particular and sectarian outlook.

The power of education can be seen to have an effect on our foreign affairs bargaining power also. In the era of cold war, where the world was bifurcated into capitalist and communist blocks, the debate was about which model of economy to operate with. In the post-cold war world now with rise in new frontiers like growth of knowledge economy flow of ideas amongst people and nations has been seen as a new yardstick of defining economic partnerships and strategic ties.

However, a word of caution here as the idea of a knowledge economy and knowledge society is different. Though with rise in the nation's integration with international regimes may lead to rise of knowledge economy, but only when its benefits trickle down to all segments with social inclusion, we have a knowledge society.

India has always been a pioneer since ancient times the in realms of mathematics with its noted Aryabhatta, science, health with its *unani* and *siddha* systems. However, when the end of knowledge is merely profit, we reach a level of stagnation. Education in local era needs redefining: this means—end relation where knowledge has to lead towards betterment of society, wisdom to appreciate the nuances of democracy and a sense of judgement over issues facing the nation.

The era of globalization is transforming the idea of culture and the values enshrined in it. The communication of information has become faster and cheaper than ever, before which indeed impacts on the social relations of a group community. Things become intricate further when we see that education has always been seen as harbinger of fostering and developing norms in a society.

Education as imparted by the family in the primitive sense is given less weightage to that by the institutions. What is essential here is that the surplus and wealth of the economic system is used to fund education without recognition of values that the very economic system enshrines. The end result is a state of confusion and uncertainty as to what should be the end path is like, once the confines of the institution are over.[2]

Though it goes without saying that information technology has made our lives better with all intriguing and absorbing aspects of the changes brought in. However, the focus of our education paradigm has to be towards non-IT realms also where we need to project areas like agriculture, research, social causes as avenues which have always been neglected by the urban educated citizenry.

The human capital of any nation is a function of its education levels and skill of the workforce. This is critical for economic growth as transformation of available inputs into desired outputs is a function of ideas only. Therefore, it shall be the quality of wealth in terms of orientation towards research and innovation and not mere emphasis on quantity that shall lead the main plank for gains in future.

There are plethora of institutions that are existing in India right now. From medicine to engineering to home sciences, you name the course and there is an institution with degrees for it. There is further chaos as to what is deemed university and college. A sad note here is we have just reduced education to mere degrees and marks here, with no special attention to student aptitude, skill development, interdisciplinary studies, amongst others.

India educational scenario is also marked by schism where the market is seen to be doing much to solve it. There is rural-urban divide, where scope for institutions in rural areas is less due to connectivity and other social barriers, the level of economic factors operationablity and community awareness is high in urban areas accompanied by the mind-sets of the society which leads to more number of private schools and colleges. There are reports which state alarming figures like five times of the rural number of children attend private educational intuitions in urban areas[3].

Our county is a land of billions where every citizen has huge aspirations. Education is always a window towards realising future dreams. Till today, when we look at school level, it is the state sector which is the major player and the private sector contributing to only 7 per cent in terms of investment. There are stories from various parts across the nation in terms of difficulties in getting access and admission to institutions. Further the demand of applicant's crosses the supply of seats. This breeds immoral practises in terms of getting seats based on approach and donations. To assume that the panacea to this problem lies in creating more schools and colleges by the state is just one part. There is a need to create an atmosphere to let private and international players come forward with integrity and confidence to take part in Indian educational growth story.[4]

New laws often create new problems which require solution. Education is a state subject in our constitution. The right to education, which has given students unimpeded promotion till secondary school certificate examination, adds to problems to the student in terms of proper orientation and the teacher in terms of workload alike as they approach higher secondary schools.[5] The problem becomes complex looking at our federal structure where we have presence of state education boards. States like Bihar lagged behind states like Kerala in terms of education which has an impact on national issues with reference to general education levels. This in turn adds another necessity for co-existing in the global era, that is, building new consultative mechanisms between the union and the states.

Universality and the concept of Equal Educational Opportunity as an objective has a few detractors. However, the education policy of the government is greatly flawed owing to the lack of standardization and quality control by various regulating authorities, and more importantly, the lack of will amongst the key players investing in this sector who want to break away from the traditional mould and create schools catering to the needs of the 21st century. So, government schools continue to plummet to great levels of despair and most private schools are 'educational-money-making-corporates.'

Diversity is becoming the key ingredient of our global lives and workforce. This heterogeneity has to be factored in by the institutions and curriculum. Most of our local issues need global solutions while global problems need help at grassroots. The education for future has to sensitize us towards this change.

Our education scenario has to focus on building up competency, retaining the talent, checking brain-drain. The need of the hour is to synchronise policy decisions with talents by taking the emphasis away from marks and grades. The pressures of external forces like globalization, technology, competition, rationalization, consolidation have made us alter our personal and professional course of action. Education patterns need to be judged by its future than the past. New competitive reality demands new roles.

The very essence of education is evolution. To negotiate the change around us brought by globalization, we cannot afford to be insular in our thoughts or actions. This industry needs dynamism, futuristic thinking, an influx of technology and a paradigm shift from a knowledge centric sector to a skill based industry model.

REFERENCES

1. Hugh Lauder & Philip Brown, *Education, Globalization and Social Change*, New York: Oxford University Press, 2006.
2. Cedric Cullingford and Stan Gunn, *Globalization, Education and Culture Shock*, Burlington, USA: Ashgate, 2005, p. xiii
3. 'Sharp Divide in Rural, Urban Education Level: NSSO Study', *The Times of India News Network*, New Delhi, 4 April 2013.
4. 'Innovation and Research to Steer India's Knowledge Economy', *The Times of India*, New Delhi, 15 February 2010.
5. 'RTE is Absolutely Foolish Policy: Manohar Parrikar', Press Trust of India, 27 May 2013.

Sandeep Jajodia

Sandeep Jajodia, who spearheads the Delhi based conglomerate 'The Monnet Group', is a man of vision and ingenuity whose focus and passion has nurtured the group from being a ferro alloy manufacturer to a fully integrated steel player having business operations in manufacturing of sponge iron, ferro alloys, steel, mining and power generation for both captive & independent power supply. As a contributing citizen, he lays great emphasis on community service and directs a significant share of his resources towards the betterment of society by running charitable schools & hospitals. An ardent sports follower, he has established Monnet Sports Foundation and adopted boxing by associating MIEL as the Official Sponsor of the Indian Boxing Team.

7

21st Century Workforce Challenges

Sandeep Jajodia

Today organizations are defining the objectives of HR keeping in mind the overall business plans and objectives. The changing context of business environment provides threats as well as opportunities for the various managerial functions. The impact of new forces like globalization on Human Resource (HR) indicates various changes like downsizing, multi-skilling, de-jobbing, which asks for changes in the traditional collective approach of human resources, wherein alongside one sees HR as a valuable asset to the organization.

It is an undoubted premise that organizations want growth and stability. HR, as an essential component of the organization, has witnessed changes in its work and features in order to contribute towards the goals and visions of the organization. For the workforce to be component and committed, the organization needs to develop new ideas for recruitment, selection, training, development.

This paper makes an attempt to understand what are the causes that have compelled the organization to come up with new ideas and answer it that HR has to undergo a qualified transition in its perspective if it has to integrate the people with the strategic goals of the organization and also manage the employees effectively.

The study begins on the fundamental premise that knowledge is essential for an innovative business mind. If business strategy has to be dynamic, it has to discuss and deliberate on the functional clauses, understand various contours of HR function and process, and juxtapose it along with the new axiom of refied perspective on HR.

This work has been divided along different paradigms—debate on nature of HR, its evolution, the changes that have come up, and in this generic analysis initiates a debate on the issue at hand that it. The ideas in various sections shall present a vision of challenges and opportunities for the human resources of the appropriate world in global times, the changing workplace reality that demands a change in thinking on what we perceive as HR.

It intends to add more to the existing HR literature and leave out new areas for debates. It seeks to enhance and upgrade the learning in HR by reflecting on various works done in the past. Lastly, the need for the work is justified along the idea that any business process has to learn and adjust as per the new insights, wherein the study intends to add a layer of a deliberative spark.

The objective of the study revolved around the central question what are the new challenges for HR? To that certain related questions were added that whether HR is sufficiently equipped in terms of the perspective through which we see the phenomena, and to add to that whether the new changes produces, are in god interest of the organization or no.

It was way back in 1996 with the remarks of Thomas Stewart that HR in its traditional mode is becoming ineffective and bureaucratic.

The people component is most essential feature of HR. Human Resource Management (HRM) is about dealing with people at work. Its core thinking is what can be done to make people more productive and satisfied. This has witnessed changes with time and the relationship has gradually evolved over the ages. In the ancient times, as seen in Greek society, there was a master-slave relation, whereas in Egyptian times, all the people worked for the pharaoh, which continued in the feudal times also in sense of relation between the vassal and the serf. With the rise of industrial society, with factors namely which Adam Smith outlined that division of labour and specialization changed the module of work. Greater efficiency in production was translated into greater profits. At the outset of the 20th century, with the help of Taylor's principles of Scientific Management, the task of management by time and motion study was to understand the best way of doing the work. With time, the focus of management shifted towards the people. HR with its focus on recruitment, selection, training, appraisals, TQM has also witnessed changes in its orientation, that of administrative expert, employee champion, change agent and strategic partner.

Whether employees are in big organization or small in number, managing them is more than just handling pay programmes, training needs, appraisals etc. In real sense, every manager in an organization is an HR manager as in some sense or the other, they engage in HR activities.

Diagnosis of what ails HR units merits an answer as to what HR professionals supposed to be—implementers or visionaries or administrators? To work with humans effectively, you need to have understanding of knowledgeable systems and practices available to us to build skilled workforce.

Every time, the role of people, as the biggest asset, is echoed by the layers of management. Organizations look after the training and development needs of the people. The vagaries of the market driven neo liberal regime often casts a doubt over continuity and stability of the job for these very assets- the people of organization.

Human resources are key to the success or failure of the organization. HRM deals with employer-employee relation management. Today many challenges are demanding comprehensive and innovative view on organization's human resources. There is great scope and potential to improve the strategy and impact of HR policies. For HRM to be successful, it cannot be left to HR specialists. There is a need for change in approach and perspective in dealing with HR, wherein the management should empathize with HR as a strategic function.

By understanding the dynamic nature of internal organizational structure and focussing on competitive external environment of the global era, there is a need to draw link connections between HR and other functions of management. Therefore, HRM in its new domain has to ensure that HR policies and activities are mutually reinforcing with that of business strategy.

The HR and the business domain is under the impact of new challenges. Outsourcing leads to organizations venture out and opt for flexible modes of work like leasing, contract employees. The conventional logic of vertical integration has now been replaced by dictum of 'lean and mean'.

Further, diversity is becoming the key ingredient of workforce whose heterogeneity the organization has to factor in. This has a direct bearing on HR and its policies.

In an attempt to extend an understanding of Strategic Human Resource, where HR policies need to be in sync with business goals, it is primarily conceptual. Sales, profits, business, production volumes, costs have been the conventional areas for the business to focus on. This emphasis on productivity was later translated into quality based performance on competitive edge.

Most HR strategies in the organization revolve around building up competency, retaining the talent, checking brain-drain. The need of the hour is to synchronise organizational decisions with talents. A common sense of grievances were found in interviews with people of few organizations questioning the strategy of the management in relation to strategic goals, compensation, development. A peculiar tendency here has been that HR is the best person to answer it.

This requires reworking, reinventing the contours of HR as talentship based on human capital as after all, 'a robust company is not a collection of leftover 'human resources.' It's a community of engaged human beings.'

Today organizations are feeling the tempo of the time- that an organization will be able to deliver to people only when the people within it are content—i.e. customer satisfaction is linked to people satisfaction. The pressures of external forces like globalization, technology, competition, rationalization, consolidation have made organizations alter their business course of action where HR is seen as integral to the process. HR patterns need to be judged by its future than the past. New competitive reality demands new roles on part of HR.

In contrast to the regular workforce, there is rise in contract personnel, consultants etc. in an effort to reduce costs. The rapidly changing technology has also made the case for upgraded learning on part of the employer and employee.

Most HR professionals struggle with the organization, in terms of their dilemma as to what contribution can they make. Some even point towards the technology boom that makes them better vigilant for the data collection and analysis of issues. It is held that it is high time HR moves beyond evaluating employees. There is a need for decision based framework that HR measurement is valuable to the extent it improves organization and management of talent. Managing payrolls, coordinating employees events, working out contracts, administrative and transactional issues have the core areas of HR work. What is interesting to note is that all this wo rk is at times done at specialist service centres, employees themselves making use of technology. This puts the onus on HR to re-module itself and search for new roles for itself.

Therefore it goes in the form of a pervasive cycle where the needs for growth and stability in a competitive environment puts the onus on the HR to transform their role from that of administrative and transactional to that of proactive approach between the organization and the individuals to synchronise their visions and aims.

Todays' organization demands speed, innovation, which in short is a much more assertive role for HR, and the focus is on traditional roles. This emphasis on HR to change itself is easier to say but strenuous to define, in reality.

There is a need for company-wide value system, upgrade competency based personnel approach, need for leadership and assessment, adequately working on compensation, ensuring workplace diversity, re-engineering the outlook on human resources. This signifies a constant re-engineering of work force role by HR managers, as that can be summed to require- In order to survive the increasing world of work, managers have to be lifelong learners.

Let us now underline what has caused the challenge for HR to redefine itself?

The term 'globalization' can be traced back to 1960s, when Marshall McLuhan foresaw that electronic dependence was creating a new form of social life, captured by the term 'global village. With demise of the Soviet Union and the subsequent withdrawal of Soviet forces from Central Europe, end of cold war, international reality also had a different trajectory of contextual forces. What has been the driving force for the human history is the ability of human condition to alter according to suit ones hopes. The webs have always channelled and co-ordinated every human action which has changed its nature to a plural tenor in present times.

Contemporary globalization has led to major reconfiguration of social geography which has affected all social structures. It has generated interplay of continuity and change, with change within their continuity rather than deeper transformations being the guiding panaroma For David Held, it is a process of 'widening, deepening and speeding up of worldwide interconnectedness in all aspects of contemporary social life.' It challenges the nation states by its supra-national forces. It is driven by international trade and finance, facilitated by communication and technology, accompanied by de-territorialization with the space-time compression.

In 1970s, the HR role was primarily seen as personnel department—to hire people, look after pay and other benefits after their work. In 1980s, the concept of 'strategic HR' was evolved where its role was enlarged to designing jobs, organization structures, compensation benefits etc. Now, it has entered the phase of competency management, acquiring talent, succession planning, system integration, amongst others, in an attempt to find, win and keep the best talent.

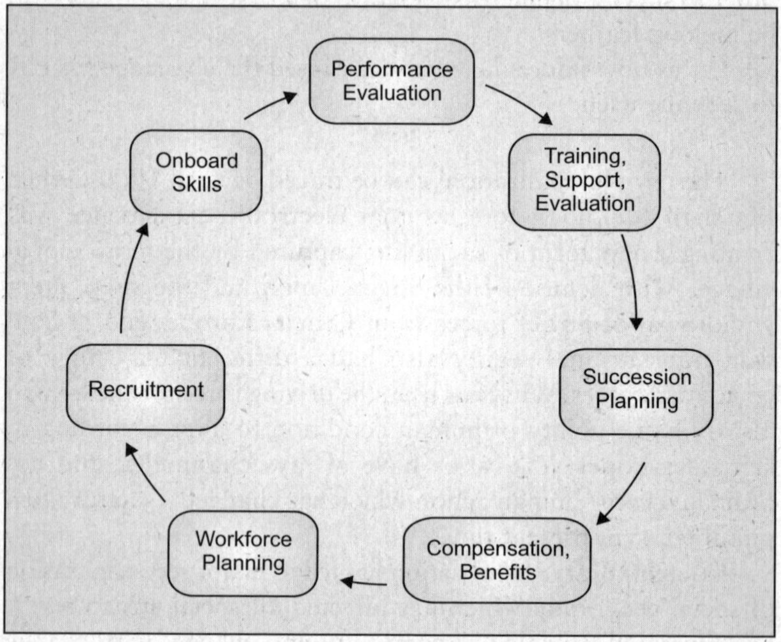

Fig. 7.1: Quest for Best Talent

Firms laying off workers, mainly for shareholder value, recession, risks being borne by workers rather than the firm, are major issues that make the employee feel insecure and less loyal to the firm. The concept of 'employee engagement' was first coined by organizational psychologist William A. Kahn in 1990. HR now to navigate between different levels- where companies have to behave in an ethical fiscally prudent manner. Though the employees are being paid to work, yet one to acknowledge their engagement along various factors like values, faith in organization ethos and the services it offers.

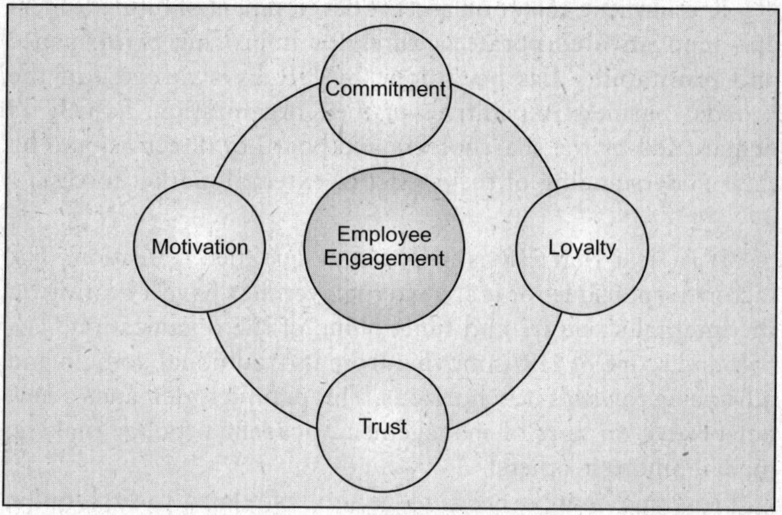

Fig. 7.2: Decline in Employee Loyalty

This aspect, along with the process of acquiring market share and customer acquisition, retention has become a complex process. How do the customers see the firm? Reliability and good employer-employee relation are defining yardsticks for organizations' image for people.

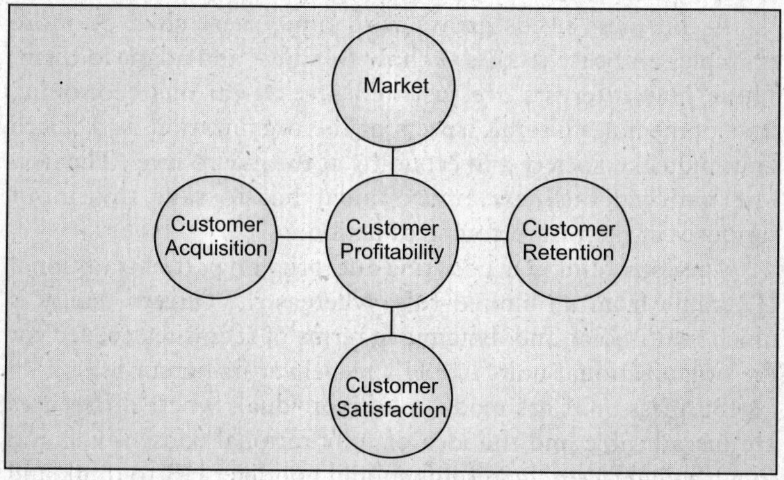

Fig. 7.3: Changing Customer Preferences

Recruitment, retention and the development of future leaders and innovative corporate cultures for improving performance and profitability has been done by HR by awareness of the broader business imperatives of their organization, namely as demarcated by the shareholders and board of directors, and by their understanding of the impact of external market forces.

It is clear that HR is in phase of qualified transition. The factors responsible for it are external, yet they have a bearing on the internal structure and functioning of the organization. The role and scope of HR is moving from its traditional domain and advancing towards new horizons. This definitely demands a new perspective on part of management, academia, policy makers, media, amongst others.

Text and context needs to be seen as related to each other, with each defining others parameters. There is no organization, which is immune from the impact of globalization. This contextual force imposes the imperative for the textual reality of HR function to redefine itself. If the organizational text shall remain the same, then a certain degree of managerial bargaining is required on part of HR professionals and consultants come into play to adapt to new forces of global integration.

As business needs grows with time, there shall be more examples and case studies on how to adjust and adapt to them. These new interests are justified due to various economic, developmental, cultural aspects of the organization as a micro unit, industry, society and economy at the macro level. The new international business environment has to take this input seriously in the future course of action.

The constraint in negotiating authority on part of traditional HR came from its limited role, whereas the current reality is much multi-polar and dynamic in terms of requisites needed for the organizational units like HR to deliver its functions.

Business units are made up of individuals where differences are ineradicable and the idea of fully rational consensus is too tough a goal to reach. Yet this should not deter HR to think and move towards its new role. Though globalization, diversity, neoliberalism are the buzzwords, yet the path towards HR in its new role may not be easy to be operationalized. However, this should not stop in the way towards evolution of HR in the global domain owing to new workplace reality.

REFERENCES

Robert L. Malthis and John H. Jackson, *Human Resource Management: Essential Perspective*, South Western Cengage Learning, Mason OH, 2012.

Dave Ulrich, *Human Resource Champions: the Next Agenda for Adding Value and Delivering Results*, Harvard Business School Press, MA, 1997.

George Bohlander and Scott Snell, *Managing Human Resources*, South Western, Cengage Learning, Mason OH, 15th Edition, 2010.

Sharon Armstrong & Barbara Mitchell, *The Essential HR Handbook*, Career Press, NJ, 2008.

Rosabeth Moss Kanter, 'Foreword', in *Human Resources in 21st Century*, eds. Marc Effron, Robert Gandossy and Marshall Goldsmith, Wily and Sons Inc, NJ, 2003

Kenneth M. York, *Applied Human Resource Management: Strategic Issues and Experiential Exercises,* Sage Publication, London, 2010.

Ralph Christensen, *Roadmap to Strategic HR: Turning a Great Idea into a Business Reality*, AMACOM books, New York, 2006.

James N. Baron & David Kreps, *Strategic Human Resources: Framework for General Managers*, John Wiley & Sons, New York, 1999.

Wayne Cascio and John Boudreau, *Investing in people: Financial Impact of Human Resources Initiatives*, Pearson Education, New Jersey, 2008.

Dr. Sujoy Shad

Dr. Sujay Shad, is an accomplished Cardiac Surgeon practicing in Delhi. He is also the pioneer surgeon who successfully commenced the heart transplant programme at Sir Ganga Ram Hospital, the first such programme in the Private sector in North India. He is also recently credited with performing the first successful Bridge to Cardiac Recovery in India using the Centrimag Left Ventricular Assist Device also known as LVAD. A gifted Cardiac Surgeon with a gentle heart, he performs more than 20 per cent of surgeries at highly subsidised rates or completely free. He has extensive research interests including in basic sciences applicable to the heart. He has developed and patented two surgical devices applicable to Cardiac Surgery including an artificial cardiac valve under development in association with various government agencies including FITT of the IIT Delhi.

8

Amidst the Cure and Curse

Dr. Sujay Shad

The importance attached to health can be understood from the common man saying 'Health is Wealth'. The attempt here is to expand the understanding of the territory of health keeping in mind new issues generated by a changing global scenario.

The Paradigm of Health

As we begin to comprehend the industry at large, it is essential to underline that healthcare is a large labour intensive industry. Health is a state subject of the Indian Constitution and the Union government only enacts laws. This often speaks about vagaries of rural versus urban health care as well as a certain lack of visible planning.

Most of us identify healthcare with large hospitals because that's the interface with a common man where healthcare directly interacts with patients or clients. One might be surprised to know that even an ordinary hospital could have up to 50 clinical departments. Quite often patients directly interact with those along with preclinical facilities and non-clinical facilities such as the i.e. hotel facilities and management structure.

In the pyramid of healthcare, tertiary healthcare occupies the pinnacle. A step lower than that would be secondary care with hospitalization for various ailments, primary care (outpatient treatments) and preventive medicine (immunization programmes, sanitation, health promotion, nutrition supplementation and accident prevention). The lower tiers of the pyramid would include pharmacy, mechanical device, bioengineering, education, research, biotechnology, drug manufacturing, drug retailers, transporters and the like.

Entry to various healthcare professional courses in India as in the world is by competitive entrance examination, including entry to medicine, nursing, physiotherapy, pharmacy, perfusion, respiratory therapy, technical apprenticeships and research. The education is time and effort intensive and makes a great foundation for time and effort intensive work that invariably follows. The base degrees are universally followed by years invested in apprenticeships or specialization which is mandatory at every level of function.

As in other industries, healthcare professionals too change their jobs; however this industry boasts high rates of staff retention. Even when people move jobs they would often remain within the confines of healthcare moving between tertiary, primary care, teaching, training, management or research.

Thus the picture that emerges from the health scenario is that highly competitive and intelligent people join their colleges and work hard towards gaining their degrees. They spend years in further training and specialization. Most healthcare professionals (HCPs) work at least 10 hours per day excluding emergency work, make extra efforts towards continuing education, teaching and research. The irony here is that the pay-out for majority of HCP's in India is suboptimal. After a threefold increase in salaries 3 years ago a senior nurse in Delhi earns ₹ 25,000/- pcm ($500) in 2013. A senior nurse usually holds a 3 year degree in nursing and has worked at least 10 years averaging 9 hours per day on a six day week. Salaries and incomes for other HCPs are similarly unsatisfactory.

Despite relatively low salaries for the intensity of work, staff retention is high and most HCP's are happy at work. That is a telling commentary about the kind of people that enter this profession, and a certain level of job satisfaction exists regardless of the remuneration. The low payment for most HCPs in our country is one of the major reasons why healthcare is cheaper compared to the more developed economies. The other reasons would be relatively less number of staff employed per patient in India and a relatively cheaper real estate (may not be true for long term if the present rate of inflation in real estate prices continues).

Major Changes have taken place in healthcare over the last ten years, and are evident across the country. Nurses' salaries for example were increased by the Government of India by almost 200 per cent in 2009; this led to a sudden exodus of nurses from the private sector to the Govt. sector. As a direct after-math the private sector was forced to follow suit to stabilize its workforce. This was followed by increased pay-outs to almost all HCPs. In turn this was funded by the paying patient. As the patient pay-outs increased so did the insurance premium. Healthcare has become more expensive over the last 10 years.

The other major change is an improved availability services across the different strata of cities. Years of public spending led to an improved infrastructure in smaller cities and towns as roads, schools, markets and malls, healthcare facilities and entertainment avenues. All these coupled with exorbitant cost of city living encouraged doctors and other healthcare professionals to settle in smaller towns, thus improving provision of services hitherto available only in larger cities. Safe conduct of complicated childbirth, basic Intensive Care Unit (ICU) setups with ventilators and Electrocardiogram (ECG) monitors, swift radiology services like ultrasound, Computed Tomography (CT) and Magnetic Resonance Imaging (MRI) scanning and others account for a trend in local provision of healthcare facilities at least in an emergency. The population living in small towns is certainly receiving improved treatments at their doorsteps.

Improved rail and road connectivity within the country now allows sick patients from remote corners to reach specialized healthcare facilities. It's not uncommon to airlift critically injured and sick patients from small airstrips in towns to metropolis for treatment. Many of these would not have reached a decent centre in the past. Critical care ambulances, evacuation of patients by trained paramedical and medical personnel by railways and air ambulances are all new to India. Safe patient transport is slowly making a difference to the outcomes of critical patients and it is heartening to see an improvement in this field. Indian ambulance networks are not yet comparable to those in the western world and are unlikely to do so in the future.

We now have a larger number of private, corporate tertiary care hospitals that are better equipped than ever before. Some 20 years ago private medicine was in its infancy in the country with very few private hospitals and most of the complicated patients would seek treatments in the larger government run hospitals and medical colleges. It is just the opposite today, most of the high end complicated work is being carried out by highly trained and motivated doctors and HCPs in the well-equipped private sector hospitals while the government run hospitals and medical colleges have considerably ceded their pre-eminence.

A gradually ageing population, a burgeoning middle class with steadily increasing incomes, improved employment avenues and associated health insurance combine to increasing healthcare demand across all towns, cities and metropolitan cities. Over the years the Indian healthcare economy appears to have grown faster than the national economy.

The Global Input

Globalization is the buzzword for increase in trade and investments which was witnessed more specifically after the global demise of socialism and triumph of capitalism after the end of Cold War. It is generally understood that great good has come of Globalization and that the Indian economy has substantially benefited.

Not everybody was overwhelmed when India moved along the liberalization spree, part of the civil society was opposed to the healthcare reforms of the structural adjustment policy. This was principally out of concern of making health an elitist good as well as service.

There were efforts made to attract more foreign investment in health owing to lack of adequate public spending, yet despite reduction of tariffs the FDI inflows have been very sluggish. FDI export however has grown, to the point that certain Indian chains now operate and own hospitals abroad.

While Indian IT and Pharmacy have returned large profits and remittances, healthcare has not lagged far behind. Today healthcare is one of fastest rising sectors with increase in cross border transactions and new business opportunities. We have an increasing number of international patients flocking to India for treatments especially surgery for chronic conditions. This is largely driven by ready availability of trained experts, large number of hospitals that are accredited by International bodies like JCI and a remarkable markdown of cost of healthcare especially in high end surgery.

There is a new notion of value buying; somebody finds value in heart surgery in India and he comes to India for treatment. Another person from India would travel to London for foetal surgery for the same reason. Value buying however, doesn't completely define globalization. To the vast majority of thinkers international health tourism is the most obvious benefit of globalization in healthcare. We would be prudent to consider globalization as increasing movement of ideas, knowledge, systems, personnel, services, equipment and money without restriction by national or even subnational boundaries.

Let's take an example here: A is a friend from college; he is a renowned psychiatrist in Munster Germany. Two other friends B and C both Paediatricians run an acclaimed charitable hospital trust in remote Chhattisgarh. All of us studied together in medical college. A visits Chhattisgarh once a year and trains paramedics to provide basic psychiatry and alcohol de-addiction services. This is charitable education directly fulfilling healthcare needs of the marginalised people, a result of globalization made possible by the feasibility of travel. On a fortnightly basis, A uses Skype to provide teaching and training to the HCPs, treats the difficult cases by providing psychotherapy and prescription drugs if required. The actions of A, vis-à-vis the services provided by B & C, too are a glimpse of globalized healthcare albeit via telecommunication.

A quarter of a century ago, when our generation was writing their thesis we would go to the library and rummage through huge dusty books called index medicus, by author, by topic and so on. Then one would go to the few medical libraries in the city hoping to find the particular journals and the references to read. No researcher today knows what is index medicus, which in its heydays was the Bible of research. At the click of the mouse today you can research your subject, find the journals online, pay online and see the particular article instantly. Thus, information technology with connectivity of the internet has become a major determinant of improving access to education in the smaller world.

Newer treatments for diseases like cancer are welcome. An unconnected doctor in the middle of nowhere might use older cancer treatment algorithms or drug dosages or drug regimens and still continue getting decent results for his patients; it is so much more common for doctors to receive alerts for new advances by online journal alerts, twitter feeds or other alerts. One can look at the most advanced treatments from the most advanced cancer trials in the world or even take part in those trials. There is now no time lag from the treatments being established in the best centres in the US, Germany or Britain to their availability and application in India.

Advanced scientific knowledge that has a direct bearing on our education, treatments and practice is truly globalized. Free movement of knowledge is the biggest boon to our healthcare by globalization; most of it thanks to advances in computing, information technology, mobile internet platforms and also by improved transportation.

Just wish to come back to value buying. We have 0.9 hospital beds per thousand populations, compared to a world average of 2.94, UK 3.0, US 3.4, Netherlands 4.7 and Switzerland 5.2. When a foreign national comes over to India for treatment and occupies a hospital bed bringing additional revenue to the treating hospital in India; the number of hospital beds per thousand native populations reduces a fraction further since a bed is taken out of the numerator (bed/population). Contrariwise, in the country of origin (of the foreign patient) the hospital bed per thousand populations would raise a tiny fraction, since the actual bed user has moved away (one less in the denominator). Sparse national resources are thereby diverted away from the local population.

This is precisely what would happen in a health system that is blindly looking at international health tourism as a revenue generator. Most Indian hospitals keen on health tourism are providing excellent service and excellent results at a fraction of the cost that the particular surgery would entail in the West. Clearly there is substantial monetary incentive for the Hospital which can often charge up to three times the rates that the domestic patient in the next bed would be paying. The international patient gets excellent treatment at a fraction of the cost that he normally would, the hospital makes three times the profit it normally would make and ditto for the doctors involved.

So who is hurt? Ask anyone who has tried to find an Intensive Care Unit (ICU) bed in any half decent hospital in Delhi. It would be surprising if an ICU bed was located in less than 5 calls. It would be even more surprising if a bed could be located in any hospital just by a phone call. A real life example given below is frightening.

A 25 years man fell from the second floor of his house 100 kms from Delhi. He sustained a major head injury with a large blood clot rapidly pressing his brain that made him unconscious. The treating doctors in the periferal city provided a first aid, started medications to slow down the speed of deterioration and placed him in an ambulance to Delhi. The panicked family started its journey to Delhi and using mobile telephones tried to reach 3 hospitals seeking emergency neurosurgery—No beds. Frantically they called relatives in Delhi who went from one hospital to another trying to find emergency neurosurgery and ICU beds. Four groups of friends and family tried a total of 7 hospitals including mine and were shown the door for lack of beds. Serendipiditiously, one of them saw me in the hospital on a Sunday afternoon, recognised me as part of the extended family and sought my help for the hurt young man who had sustained a major head injury with one-sided dilated pupil. This clearly was a situation where nothing short of a major neurosurgery would offer a shot at life and whether the outcome would be an alive healthy person, or an alive and crippled or vegetative person was unknown. I went to the casualty and was told the same 'no beds'. I called up a friendly Neurosurgeon and demanded that the lad be admitted in the OT if there was no bed, be kept there and recovered there if nothing else was forthcoming and that he must be operated. He underwent a lifesaving surgery in the next 30 minutes, started opening his eyes by five days, started moving a limb every fifth day. A month after his accident he left hospital in a fully functional condition. He is working full time now four months after his miraculous day at our hospital. Had I, a hospital insider not been there, or if they had failed to recognise me or if I had accepted a no as a no would he not have died in the ambulance going from one door to another? In a better system, a neurosurgeon would await this patient with the operation theatre at the ready. Unfortunately we are short of beds, staff and facilities to cope with the healthcare needs of our people.

For that matter this lad occupied a bed for 30 days and by doing so he was the reason behind 20 people with appendicitis, cholecystitis, malaria or even a head injury got turned away from my hospital.

Till such time that we are physically short of hospital beds for the local population, is it appropriate for us to tom tom our healthcare abroad and seek rich dividends? Ofcourse if we are no longer a service and use the euphesim of an industry then profiteering from healthcare globalization is unquestionably acceptable. We don't even need to make an attempt to camouflage this greed and denial of the basic rights of the marginalised in our society.

Over the coming years, we shall have more internationally accredited hospitals and increasing traffic of international health tourists. The Indian private hospital chains are adding to their bed strength at a rapid pace and aggressive recruitment strategies are employed to gain and retain the best clinicians. Since there was no work force planning for healthcare over the last decades, we are faced today with a dearth of suitably qualified and trained personnel. One could envisage a situation where a hospital building cannot be staffed because of personnel shortage.

To meet those needs, returning NRI doctors and senior faculty from teaching hospitals will be attracted with liberal salary packages and other incentives to join the private medical chains. The same will be true for other healthcare associated businesses whether pharma, research or otherwise. For the suitably educated, qualified and experienced people at long last there would shortly be avenues and incentives in India; something to look forward to.

Interestingly, people of only Indian descent can work and earn a salary in the healthcare arena; I was horrified to learn this since I had learned and earned from the UK. One of my former British associates was enticed by two major hospital chains to work in India and requested to join as Chief of Cardiac Surgery. When the deal suffered a rough patch, my worried associate requested me to look into the matter. A few days later I stumbled upon the rules and regulations of the Medical Council of India which totally forbids any non-Indian to earn money by practising medicine in India. I felt like a crook, who benefited from the liberal British system where you are paid for the job you do; when my own country doesn't allow any such facility. Regardless of this sudden humiliation, when I look at the workforce shortfall due in India, this would be greatly advantageous to the 'Indian' doctors who would be in a buyers market.

In the coming times better salary packages for all HCPs will be the norm in big cities and smaller tier 2 or 3 cities. Those smaller cities have been the focus of primary healthcare until 10 years ago; they are going to be the arena for a major growth of specialities in the coming years. For the younger people in healthcare a well thought plan should not miss out on the opportunities in the smaller cities.

Medical colleges and Government Institutes would continue to face exodus of trained faculty and be starved of good teachers and trainers. Medical education in the countries' premier medical colleges could come under a strain.

For the corporates trying to set up and manage new units in smaller cities there will be the usual challenges, albeit with easier HCP recruitments and welling coffers. Patients in smaller cities would get improved access to organised private healthcare, certainly at a rising cost. Health insurance industry should continue to blaze thorough record enrolments.

Vedabhyas Kundu

Vedabhyas Kundu is Programme Officer at Gandhi Smriti and Darshan Samiti, Ministry of Culture, Government of India. His area of specialization is media literacy, children and media, peace and conflict resolution and volunteerism. He has written on different aspects of media literacy and how it can be used to promote peace orientation among young people. He has also written extensively on volunteerism in different books published by international organizations like United Nations Volunteers.

9

Globalized World : A Boon for Media Literacy

Vedabhyas Kundu

Introduction

New Media in My Life

I am a village girl. I am doing my plus one education in Wayanad, Kerala. I am also doing my communication training in an organization. From there I have realized the potential of the new media. What we couldn't do person to person, I realized that with the help of the new media we can do far better. For example, I travel rarely outside my district, but with the help of a blog or social media I can communicate with people around the world.

If used in the proper way I am sure we can learn more from the new media, we can connect with individuals and organizations beyond our geographical boundaries. From my personal experience I have observed how effectively the official blog of the centre and social networks, like Facebook, shared inspirational stories of education to the world. Through our newspaper, *The Peace Gong* we are able to exchange stories from friends in different parts of India and abroad. For instance, our friend in Pakistan, Syeda Rumana Mehdi's poems have been inspiring us to think of conflicts around the world. We discuss some of these issues like how children are getting affected by the Syrian crisis and how we can end conflicts in our own communities. We have been extensively using our 'The Peace Gong' group in the Facebook for connecting with like minded students.

Also using the new media, we children of the Wayanad Shishu Panchayat are trying to connect with other Shishu Panchayats across the country and aiming to create a national movement. We feel elated when we are able to develop programmes simultaneously in Kerala, Assam, Karnataka, Tripura and West Bengal; we have spoken to children in these states using Skype from our respective centres. We use mobile phones to call our seniors for guidance. We also use SMS to reach out to friends and acquaintances on the work we are trying to do in the village. Who says we are different from our friends in the cities? It has changed our perspectives and the whole way we are trying to work in the community.

The new media is a great tool of education. It helps to make the technological advancements a creative process. When we design and upload in our blogs, as a student interested in creative pursuits, it gives me immense pleasure and at the same time I am also happy that I, as an obscure village girl, is being noticed by the world even beyond oceans.......

> Thansila, 16 and President of the Wayanad Shishu Panchayat is the editor of the Malayalam edition of the *Peace Gong*, the global children's newspaper (she had originally written this in Malayalam and has been translated by her adult coordinators).

For young people like Thansila, who come from backward communities, the exponential growth of media is opening up new opportunities to connect with others in different parts of the country and abroad. Thansila's account of how children like her are using the new media to connect with others across the country and abroad is a reflection of the globalization process which, according to Tomlinson (1997), 'shrinks the concepts of distance between existing cultures by dramatically reducing the time taken to cross distances that physically separate them'.

Two important theories of media globalization are aptly reflected by Thansila's perspectives. Even though she rarely travels beyond her district, Wayanad in Kerala, she is in touch with friends around the world through the blog, 4righteducation.blogspot.in and also use of social networking sites like Facebook. She tells how she and her friends are inspired by their Pakistani friend's poems on conflicts.

Marshal McLuhan's concept of 'the global village' pertinently describes how the new media technology has penetrated even in interior areas which help village girls like Thansila connect with others across the world. However, McLuhan's idea of homogenized global village may not be apt to describe the efforts of young people like Thansila and their cultural transformations while using the media. In this context, use of concepts like 'glocalization', which talks of the convergence of global and local, could possibly be more appropriate.

When Thansila describes how she and members of Wayanad *Shishu Panchayat* discuss how children in the Syrian conflict are affected and try to evolve dialogues on conflicts within their own communities, it reflects Giddens arguments on the tensions between globalization and localizations. He describes globalization as 'the intensification of the world-wide social relations which link distant locations in such a way that local happenings are shaped by events occurring many miles away and vice versa'.

Thansila's perspectives form the foundation of this chapter which will try to capture different dimensions of the impact of the globalizing media. As she says that the new media has helped her, an obscure village girl, 'to be noticed by the world even beyond oceans', it talks of the transformative nature of the media. In this context, Tornero and Varis (2010) have opined that the new hypertechnological environment, the deepening of communicative globalization, has not only altered the way we perceive and use time and space, it has also changed the chemistry of our everyday life and our culture'. It is also important to note that as distinction between different media forms, like television, radio, press, books, telephone and computers, is shrinking the citizenry has to engage with a media culture that is all-pervasive and intensive.

The chapter will not only try to analyse how advancement of media technology in the globalized media scenario is giving citizens like Thansila the wherewithal to access media, it will also try on the other hand to delve on how the unabated commodification of the media is also responsible for what eminent journalist P Sainath describes the 'disconnect between the mass media and the masses'. While it will look at the issue of formation of identities in today's media architecture, as a solution on how the citizenry can negotiate the new complexities arising from the ubiquitous media environment, it would argue on the importance of furthering media literacy education.

Some Perspectives on the Indian Media today

The exponential growth of the media in India in recent years, which enables children like Thansila to use these communication tools, is captured by Ninnan (2011) who opines that twenty years after the economic liberalization process began in India the increased growth of advertising in the country has led to more media and greater media access for the average citizen, including those who cannot read. The country now has more than 700 satellite channels and several thousand publications. Along with this increase are the phenomenal growth of mobile telephony and the reach of Internet connectivity.

Jain (2011) accentuates Ninan's arguments as he talks of how the Indian media has grown at an unprecedented rate in the last 20-25 years. Notwithstanding the fact that many ordinary Indians like Thansila are able to access different communication tools much more easily than about a decade back, the flip side is the overwhelming commercialization and commodification of the media itself. Jain (2011) notes that large sections of the media have adopted the market as the ultimate arbiter of everything they do, if they succeed in reaching larger audiences, they are doing what the market wants, not only is the news a product to be sold to audiences, the news space is also a product to be sold to advertisers, be they be of corporate interests or of politicians. This unrestrained pursuit of profit has led to an abandonment of the media's role as an ethically credible watchdog in matters of governance and democracy.

In fact the rapid changes in the Indian media scenario; especially the phenomenal expansion of television channels, the entry of foreign media and expansion of Indian media abroad can be linked to the watershed year of 1991. Ninnan (2006) for instance points out that in 1991 some of the big media companies either did not exist then or were cottage industries. These could be linked to the opening up of the economy following the economic liberalization process in 1991 (Abhijit Bannerjee, 2006).

Bhaskara Rao et al., (2005) argues that with big money involved in the running of the media industry, 'advertising, market research and media planning sets the scope and pace of media including the case of ownership pattern and journalistic trends.' J.V. Vilanilam (2005) taking forward the discourse on how the media industry has shaped up post-1990s observes that the 'media seems to have only one goal and that is to deliver the maximum number of readers, viewers and listeners to the advertiser'.

Here it needs to be pointed out that the changes in the Indian media are in line with the global scenario, the globalization of the mass media. McCannon (2009) argues that it is an era in which the world's most dominant organizations are the media cartel and their major advertisers. They drive relentlessly for profit, overwhelming busy parents, teachers, counsellors, and preachers. Daily, we create a historic new social experiment with the health of children and democracy. As mainstream media merge into ever larger global conglomerates, advertiser-approved content expands to the exclusion of less profitable, prosocial programming for children and quality news for citizens, he says.

Meanwhile Tehranian (2002) points out that three technological trends characterize the global media, including digitalization, convergence, and miniaturization. The technological transformations have led to three structural consequences, namely, globalization, localization, and fragmentation. Structural changes have in turn led to three new cultural patterns, including transnationalization, tribalization, and democratization.

Thussu (2000) talks of how entry of global media conglomerates opened up a new visual world for Indian audiences. Guha Thakurta (2012) argues that in the last few years there has been a growing consolidation of media organizations across the globe. In the political economy of the media the world over there is clearly an alarming absence of not-for-profit media organizations, he adds.

The changing structures of Indian media and the ownership patterns have also made a major impact on the media content. For instance in television, not only there is easy availability of western-based programmes, but even many local programmes follow formats of their western counterparts. Of course there are local variants and flavour to all of such programmes. Even in children's programme segments, a host of cartoon films made in the US, Japan etc are available dubbed in local languages. Here it would be important to note that there are different perspectives to the extent of cultural influence many of these formats have on local contents. While one group of scholars describe these as aspects of cultural imperialism furthered by the western countries, another group of scholars observe that this analysis in the context of imperialism is outmoded. They rather try to explain it as a more complex process using the Gramscian perspective of hegemony. Wong (2006) in this context notes as the cultural influence of the North has been internalized or rationalized by the South ... for their adoption of the programme concept and format implies some dominance at work via consensus building inherent in the hegemonic influence.

While these trends give space to wide range of diversity of options in different media forms available to the audience today, the commodification of the mass media tends to expose the people constantly to new dimensions of neo-liberal ideas and doctrines carefully packaged for consumption. They have become passive consumers of media messages having difficulties in discerning between fact and fiction. This facet of media globalization strives to promote Strinati's (1995) features of postmodernism which talks about emphasis on style over substance.

Identity Formation

This takes us to an important aspect of the media globalization process–the formation of identities. The heightened influence of the new convergent media on the globalization influences the socio-cultural identities of individuals using these tools. Hamley (2008) points out that with multiple examples of identity found in the media, now fuelled by the digital media, people will have difficulty in distinguishing between these examples.

According to Chen (2012) the convergence of new media and globalization brings about at least six new experiences for human beings, including new textual experiences, new ways of representing the world, new relationships between users and new media technologies, new conceptions of the biological body's relationship to technological media, and new patterns of organization and production. These experiences, Chen says, will inevitably challenge the traditional formation and definition of social or cultural identity.

In this context, Belay (1996) argues that the new cultural identity formed by new media may not change the traditional meaning of cultural identity as a unique product through interaction in a specific group context, which gives members a sense of belongings to the group, but it will directly challenge the traditional attributes of cultural identity; namely–temporality, territoriality, constrastivity, interactivity, and multiplicity.

Clothier (2005) talks of a hybridized cultural identity which can emerge from being inducted into a virtual community composed of diverse people and cultural influences that border and overlap each other. However, there are scholars who have challenged this notion of hybrid identities arguing that in reality it is the hegemonic western culture which has the power advantage in the formation of cultural identities.

Importance of Media Literacy

The contention and contestation on the impact and use of a globalized media environment takes us to the importance of promoting media literacy amongst the citizery. Critical consciousness and understanding of the media is important to make the best possible use of the new media environment. It is in this context, that media literacy, especially when it involves digital literacy and information literacy becomes, important.

The importance of media education was underlined by the UNESCO Declaration on media education or also called the Grunwald Declaration which says that 'the school and the family share the responsibility of preparing the young person for living in a world of powerful images, words and sounds. Children and adults need to be literate in all three of these symbolic systems and this will require some reassessment of educational priorities.' The contemporary notion of media education is based on concepts of 'critical awareness', 'democratic participation' and even 'enjoyment of the media'. (Buckingham *et al.,* 2001)

Tornero *et al*., (2010) stress that media literacy should offer concepts, rules and competences to help people to properly use the information disseminated by the media. Arguing that media literacy is closely tied to problem-solving methodology, Tornero observes it should help in development of capacities of various skills like creative skills, communicative skills, semiotic and cultural skills, and operative skills (technical skills needed to use the technologies and media).

They note that the 'information and knowledge society is demanding new methods for processing and producing information, which will be sought through collective intelligence and the network society, and new languages that will come through the language of interaction with technology and communication'.

For young people today, Tornero *et al*., call for a 'new media literacy curriculum which could provide the right language for interacting with technology, a language that enables the subject, the person, to have sufficient autonomy and trains them properly to inhabit and live in an increasingly absorbing media and technological environment. According to them, media literacy 'entails the acquisition of a new culture in which technology and human beings are in harmony with and complement one another.

Renee Hobbs (1998) articulates on the importance of media literacy education. She notes that media literacy practices helps strengthen students' information access, analysis and communication skills and build an appreciation for why monitoring the world is important. Media literacy can inform students about how the press functions in a democracy, why it matters that citizens gain information and exposure to diverse opinions, and why people need to participate in policy decision-making at the community, state and federal levels. Secondly, media literacy can support and foster educational environments in which students can practice the skills of leadership, free and responsible self-expression, conflict resolution and consensus building, because without these skills, young people will not be able to effectively engage with others in the challenges of cooperative problem-solving that participation in a democratic society demands. Third, media literacy skills can inspire young people to become more interested in increasing their access to diverse sources of information.

Meanwhile, Kumar (2007) has tried to give this perspective more relevance for developing countries like India when he argues that the primary goals of media education are the conscientization, empowerment and liberation of the community and of society as a whole. Its concerns are the promotion of equality, social justice, democracy, freedom, human dignity and a more humane society. The methods or strategies it employs are mainly, dialogue, reflection and action.

Notwithstanding the goals and aims of media literacy education as discussed above, it can be noted that much of media education as taught in Indian Universities and institutions of mass communication purely cater to the needs of the media industry. Students coming out of these institutions confirm to the neo-liberal orientations of these media organizations.

In this context, it would be important to encapsulate the goals of media literacy in a diverse country. It would be pertinent if media literacy education enables the citizenry to develop capacities to negotiate the complexities of a convergent media architecture and be able to critically understand the underlying influences of hegemony.

To conclude, Nagaraj and Kundu (2013) argue that the framework for media and information literacy (MIL) education in India should encompass the deep-rooted cultural tradition, pluralism and significance of mutual respect and nonviolence. They stress that training in MIL should help facilitate dialogue between diverse communities, further positive engagement in conflict situations, promote a culture of peace and, most importantly, facilitate sustainable development. This goal of media literacy is aptly reflected by Iflah Javed Qureshi, a class XII student from Srinagar and Editor of the children's newspaper, *The Peace Gong*:

"Our newspaper, *The Peace Gong* promotes diversity and helps in facilitating dialogues amongst young people from different cultures and communities. We extensively use the social media, email communications and mobiles to connect with other student reporters from different backgrounds across the country and abroad. Using new forms of available communication, *The Peace Gong* can be a powerful vehicle to help young people to come together and work for global peace."

REFERENCES

Bannerjee, A. (2006). Diversity and innovation through competition. http://www.india-seminar.com.

Belay, G. (1996). The (Re)construction and negotiation of cultural identities in the age of globalization. In H. B. Mokros (Ed.), *Interaction & identity*. New Brunswick, NJ: Transaction, pp. 319-346.

Chen, Guo-Ming (2012). The impact of new media on intercultural communication in global context; *China Media Research*; 8.2, April 2012.

Giddens, A. (1990). The consequences of modernity. Oxford: Polity Press.

Hamley, Catherine (2008). Media Use in Identity Construction; http://aber.ac.uk.

Hobbs, R. (1998). Building citizenship skills through media literacy education in M Salvador and P Sias (Eds), *The Public Voice in a democracy at risk*. Westport, CT: Praeger Press.

Jain, Savyasaachi (2011). The Mediatization of Politics and 'Paid News' in

India. In Namaste published by Prasar Bharati to mark the 48th General Assembly of the Asian Broadcasting Union; November 2-8, 2011.

Kumar, K. J. (2007). Media Education, Regulation and Public Policy in India; Paper presented at the UNESCO Paris Conference on Media Education.

McCannon, R. (2009). Media Literacy/Media Education. Solution to Big Media in *Children, Adolescents and the Media*. Sage Publications.

Nagaraj, K. V. & Kundu, Vedabhyas (2013). The Role of Media and Information Literacy in promoting Mutual Respect and Sustainable Development in Culturally Diverse India; In Media and Information Literacy and Intercultural Dialogue, ed. Ulla Carlsson and Sherri Hope Culver; MILID Yearbook 2013; the International Clearinghouse on Children, Youth and Media; Nordicom, University of Gothenburg.

Ninan, Sevanti (2011). Media Growth, Development and Inequality. In Namaste published by Prasar Bharati to mark the 48th General Assembly of the Asian Broadcasting Union; November 2-8, 2011.

Ninnan, T. N. (2006). The Changing Indian Media scene; ; http://www.india-seminar.com/2006/561; Media Matters, Seminar, May 2006.

Rao, Bhaskara. N. and Vasanti, P. N. (2005). Media Scene as India Globalises. Centre for Media Studies.

Strinati, D. (1995). *An Introduction to Theories of Popular Culture*. London: Routledge.

Tehranian, Majid (2002); Peace Journalism: Negotiating Global Media Ethics; Presented at the PCC: Peace, Culture and Communications Commissions; IPRA General Conference in South Korea.

Thussu, Daya Kishan (2000). Indian Media- from colonial to global? Imperium, volume 1, December 2000; http://imperiumjournal.com.

Tomlinson, J. (1997). Cultural Globalization and Cultural Imperialism. In A Mohammadi (Ed.), *International Communication and Globalization*. London, Thousand Oaks & New Delhi, Sage Publications.

Tornero, J. M. Perez & Varis, Tapio (2010). Media Literacy and New Humanism; UNESCO Institute for Information Technologies in Education.

Vinalinam, J. V. (2005). *Mass Communication in India: A Sociological Perspective*; Sage Publications.

Wong, Kokkeong (2006). Beyond Domination and Interdependency. In Globalization Through The Media; Paper for presentation at the 15th AMIC Annual Conference, "Media in Asia: Aspirations, Choices and realities," held in Penang, Malaysia, on 17-20 July, 2006.

http://4righteducation.blogspot.in.

Archana B Sapra

Delhi based professionally qualified architect and independent arts consultant Archana B Sapra is co-founder of Arts4All Trust—an NGO that aims to promote dialogue across cultures and bridge the gap between the folk and contemporary, while promoting excellence through an exchange of ideas and innovation within the visual arts. She is also on the editorial board for 'Creative Mind' quarterly art magazine. She has curated several exhibitions for different art institutions, including CrossOver—a residency and exhibition at Dhaka and Delhi for artists from India and Bangladesh and Merging Metaphors an India ASEAN artists' residency and exhibition. She was also the project consultant for a multi arts festival in Delhi and researcher for '5000 Years of Indian Art' book.

10

Contemporary Indian Art Scenario: An Overview

Archana B Sapra

Indian Art and aesthetics, traced back to an over 5000 years old civilization with depth, richness and diversity, is rooted in a pluralistic society. The multitude of contemporary Indian artistic expressions mirroring the country's enormous ethnic, linguistic, geographical, political and cultural diversity, continues to draw on the ancient philosophical principles of *Shilpasatras* and classical traditions of the sacred and the courtly as well as its tribal and folk forms. It also incorporates newer influences of media and technological innovations. Incredible India, many 'India-s' in one, is a multicultural 'Glocal' world or local and global, as is exemplified in expressions of visual art and other tangible or intangible creative art forms such as literary works and performances.

Arts involve application of human imagination and creative skills and artists create work for self-expression and communication. Visual artists in India since times immemorial continue to paint sculpt and design temple statutory and other objects for rituals, worship and decoration. They make earthen pots for cookware, textiles and jewelery for body adornment, and other craft and art objects for everyday use and aesthetic enhancement of their surroundings.

The Current Indian Art Scape

The opening up of the economy, all pervasive impact of information technology, melting down of barriers and ease of travel, more so since the turn of the century, have changed the face of the land and its arts scape. It has not only opened up the horizon but also facilitated an interface between the local and global, helping Indian art develop as an eclectic mix of the old and the new with a high level of sophistication. Skills continue to be passed on from father to son over generations, for traditional folk and tribal creations that reflect rootedness of the Indian art. Contemporary expressions in multifarious modes and media highlight the merging of art/craft/ design/technology and high and low art, floating between art created for traditional utilitarian purposes and those targetted for upscale gallery precincts.

Indian art today adorns different styles, shades and shapes of paintings, sculptures, installations, photography, graphic art, site specific and ephemeral work, conceptual, project based, performance art, design, craft, cuisine, films, fashion, advertising, digital, animation and video art, and works in other media. The art scene has undergone an unprecedented surge in appreciation, for its intrinsic merit as well as rapidly growing market value, both nationally and internationally. Given its reach and output, the numbers of people it engages and the turnover it goes through, directly and indirectly, including the ancillary businesses and its socio-economic impact, art and culture business in India has assumed the status of an industry.[1]

There is a growing significance and presence of Indian art in today's networked world. Many young contemporaries have gained a foothold in the global art scenario, juggling and experimenting with media, materials and modes, and using latest technologies. Comfortably floating across different socio-cultural-economic domains, rural and urban, and the decorative and the provocative, they engage with an amalgam of different micro-worlds. Not just the metros, but also the smaller Indian cities are experiencing the ripples of the growing interest in art. With galleries and art colleges coming up in far-flung areas such as Jharkhand and Kochi, young artists find it exciting and profitable to engage in art. There is a leveling of the playing fields with women entering the art domain and merging of art, craft and design, or low, high and popular art. Artists of all shapes and varieties, art galleries, studio spaces, residencies, art material suppliers, lighting, graphic and display designers, framers, academics, experts, photographers, curators, museums, nonprofit institutions, auction houses, banks, financiers, art fairs, critics, consultants, managers, historians, collectors and their advisors to name a few-work together to make the contemporary Indian art scene click.

The global interface has also expedited the merging of the different streams of creativity. There are visual art works that incorporate music, dance, drama, lights, sound, literature and other artistic media to make a creative potpourri that is dynamic and mellifluous. The porosity of boundaries with exchanges and ease of travel, has been wide spread beyond the traditional interests in the West to spread across Africa and Asia reinforcing historic cultural affinities, though in a newer context. The emergence of regional art and artists from smaller towns has caught the attention of cultural theorists and art historians.

With free access to information and instant communication across countries and continents turning a reality, given the wide reach of the Internet, local artists are able to access exhibitions, publications and other visual material in the same time frame as their western counterparts, with the size of the audience growing simultaneously. The erosion of geographical boundaries has also helped the formation of new groupings and enjoined communities with shared interests and ideas, rather than by location, altering the face and colour of Indian art.

There is enhanced acceptability of diversity and engagement with education and exchange through art. Since art is a universal language that touches the heart and the mind, it can be used effectively to communicate even complex ideas and issues to the young and the old, the intellectual and the illiterate. This power of the arts to critique has occasionally been though perceived as a threat by the state resulted in curbing the freedom of expression as in the case of MF Hussain. The trade-off between freedom of expression and limits of liberal democracy were witnessed in the way his exhibitions were wrecked, and demonstrations against his work held. His death in a foreign land, where he was pushed to live in a self-imposed exile, puts a question mark on the credibility of a state as impartial and its ability to enforce law and order[2] and guarantee fundamental right of all citizens, under Article 19(2) of the constitution.[3]

Despite such aberrations, Indian artists bustling with energy are creating work bordering on the radical and the provocative. Willing, and increasingly now able to afford taking risks; the new generation is experimenting with multiple and unconventional forms as they head towards renewal and regeneration. New cutting edge media is coming to the forefront, even as traditional media continues to pulsate. The work features current history and events. Artists respond to personal concerns and human issues around strife and violence. Their art addresses a spectrum of socio-political and environmental themes with aesthetic insight and intellectual depth. It also reflects on the rapid changes altering the face and culture of new globalized cities and their lack of cohesive social fabric.

The Global Impact

The trajectory of globalization in an interface with art presents an interesting dichotomy. Both notions are complex and continuous, ideas in progress, as on-going debates. However, while globalization tries to develop a system where human species are ordered along the logic of a single system; arts do not adhere to such a stable perception. Deep thoughts and inkling of a lurching mind are its basis.[4]

In fact, the idea of free movement has existed since the era of the silk route. The end of cold war; followed by the rise of information technology made people connected and undivided by time and space hurdles. The current neo-liberal times may present the idea of 'global' cutting across borders in new and unique ways, but the realm of Art has been global throughout.

In transgressing borders it conveys messages and translates ideas, tapping into diversity, which the current global focus is increasingly trying to tap.

In this context the exposure that Indian art and artists have had to international audiences through art fairs, exhibitions, workshops, exchanges, residencies, museum shows, collaborations, dialogues, travels, books, publications, reproductions and the Internet, has had a positive two way impact. The travels and exchange of art and artists from across the world, has not only taken Indian art abroad but also brought overseas art and artists to the country, dissolving cultural barriers and making them global citizens. Technological inventions and interventions of the last couple of decades have spilled over into the way art is made, exhibited and received. Spoilt for choice, Indian artists, like their counterparts elsewhere, create work on unprecedented scale, as their creativity is no longer confined to paint brush canvas.

The rules of the game are also being re-written and reshaped. The notion of beauty and the definition of art, its scale and scope, the way of making, looking and presenting and collecting it- are all constantly in a flux, being renegotiated. In a collage of styles, substances and new media artists are seen to give a free play to their imagination. They create art with help from assistants. Some of their studios appear more like industrial and factory assembly lines, blurring the divide between art and technology.

The enhanced global circulation of Indian art through biennales and triennials has brought the local into global focus. The artistic spectacle, Indian in content and transnational in its imaging and scale, such as Subodh Gupta's use of water tumblers and other kitchen utensils for installation titled *Very Hungry God*; that are presented at such forums, turn things inside out, bringing national culture and concerns onto an international stage and reach an expanded audience. International museums and galleries are interested in setting up shop in India and supporting innovative collaborative art ventures.

Art Market

The Indian art and its market value, that created ripples in the 1990s, continues to draw international attention for the extraordinary level of resistance that it is able to offer, despite the general context of ongoing global financial crisis and its somewhat unorganized nature. Fortune magazine, had reported it as the fourth most-positive art market in the world with 485% rise in the last decade. A subsequent survey put India's share in the global art market at $250 million, which though stays at less than 1% of the total global art market estimated at worth $60.8 billion. There is scope and need to do more.

The general financial melt down, has clearly impacted the Indian art market, too. Fortunately though there are several positive indicators that suggest a resistant scene. One of these is the support and input of private galleries, and enterprises and the other, emergence of a new class of collectors. An increasing number of upper-middle-class upwardly mobile Indian professionals and entrepreneurs, besides the old-time wealthy Indian connoisseurs, have been buying art. These high net-worth individuals have helped sustain the market. They buy not only the established artists work but also acquire new media creations by the young and unknown, for their aesthetic appeal and investment as an alternative asset class. The increased awareness of Indian art, not just the classical but also contemporary art, by masters as well as emerging star artists, has also fuelled their popularity leading to an exponential growth in the prices of their work. Many of them sell for record-breaking prices in prestigious auctions conducted by Christies and Sotheby in London and New York.

The art industry has grown and evolved at various levels in recent years.[5] Several private museums and art institutions such as Kiran Nadar Museum of Art and Devi Art Foundation have come up, bringing Indian art into the public domain. In art education, the School of Art & Aesthetics at Jawaharlal Nehru University (JNU) has taken a lead. Art awards instituted by non-profit organizations, e.g. *Sanskriti*, offer new opportunities for innovation and creation. There is a mushroom growth of art galleries in several Indian cities, and there are professional agencies that provide art-related services, including handling, packing, transportation, insurance, framing, display, care and conservation of art and they are doing brisk business.

Art professionals advising on the selection, provenance, authentication, exhibition design, and curation of art exhibits, for a fee, are much in demand. Art perceived as a wealth asset; is increasingly being managed by corporates, bankers, and finance-professionals. Hedge funds and auction houses such as Saffron Art have jumped into the fray. Such attempts serve twin purpose, while creating awareness amongst the public about the country's artistic talents and milieu, they also connect collectors with art, giving them an opportunity to procure original works.[6] Evidently, contemporary artists, galleries, cultural and support institutions, all those working in marketing, public relations, media and art affiliates have undergone unprecedented shifts. There is competition in the market and the industry is attracting talent. It is a source of livelihood to an estimated 265 million artists and skilled and semiskilled artisans from across the country and to a million others engaged in the ancillary businesses, services and facilities.

This exposure, economic development, and technological advancement; though have helped the art scene and art market grow, in terms of its quality, quantity and reach; it has simultaneously sparked some social economic and cultural tensions. Many of the transactions done in cash support of a parallel economy and the operations are not always handled in most transparent manner. The search for fresh ideas and new markets also presents a paradox as artists are seen to struggle to retain their unique ethos and identity, while trying to conform to western tastes and templates, as did some of the miniaturists and Kalighat painters during the Company period.

The corporatization of contemporary Indian art as an industry has helped it find space and recognition in the global scenario. Locally though, it remains somewhat isolated from the vast milieu as the dynamics of art commerce are allowed to lead the path, to the detriment of the society at large. Another drawback, given the pulls of commercialization, is the prime focus on art as an investment rather than for its aesthetic quality. This lopsided emphasis has adversely affected the art scene and the surrounding infrastructure.

Galleries are often focusing more on artists whose works sell. They goad them into doing decorative and repetitive work; as some of the investor-collectors prefer to go by the market trends and popularity of the artists rather than the inherent merit of the works. Museums, too, try to play safe and hesitate to support experimental work. Art magazines funded and owned by galleries and commercial institutions publish only such articles and reviews that befit their business interests. And there are critics who write about art and artists from a more subjective perspective rather than express their independent and objective points of view, impacting the whole process of artistic creation, critique and dissemination. Prices of art works are calculated on per square foot formula as if they were standardized factory products. The relative autonomy of art field appears threatened in the face of indiscriminate corporatization of market models and values with a focus on public relations or PR and box office.

In market economies, state funding for arts has been a contentious matter. It is of concern for the federal and state government alike in the United States of America, while budgetary constraints are restricting the developments in arts field in the United Kingdom and Italy too.[7] In India, the Ministry of Culture, at the Union level, covers the realm of art with a limited budget, given the governments focus on sectors like health, education, and defense. Private sector spending on art is also minimal with most sponsors preferring to divert their funds towards other zones like sports and movies. Entrenched in the idea of 'increasing material wealth' profit margins and turnovers, sponsors are ever ready to spend large sums of money on big budget films initiatives, that regretfully over shadow all other forms of arts—classical, folk and tribal forms. Clearly the pressures of market and issues of funding have created existential and survival crisis for the latter.[8]

Conclusion

Despite some challenges, the strong Indian presence of Indian art in galleries, exhibitions, auction houses and affiliated industries in the country and internationally, has undoubtedly helped generate direct economic benefits for the artists, the society and country. Indian art and culture industry employs a large number of people. Backed by a positive socio-economic environment, and conducive policies, involving public-private partnership, the art sector can be an effective driving force also for tourism industry. Its impact on tourism can be seen and felt in the way cities like Edinburgh, through its annual Festival and the Basel with its Art Fair, bring in thousands of visitors to the region. Besides such art projects also expand the cultural and artistic opportunities available to the residents and increase the visibility of their cities as tourist destinations on the global map.

Art has clearly enhanced Indian image worldwide, working as an effective tool for diplomatic influence, and an epitome of our culture, values and ethos. However, most of this has been done through private initiatives. The government has lagged behind in supporting and investing in art and culture. Public funding and official support is essential to take the movement forward and provide it stability. Organized exchange with major museums in other countries, corporate patronage for enhancing local museum collections, showcasing foreign artists' work in India, and building suitable infrastructure for art are some of the tasks that government can take a lead on, to help Indian art take center stage on world map.[9]

REFERENCES

1. Rajeev Sethi, 'Fast Forward—The Future of India's Creativity', The Planning Commission, Government of India, 2008.
2. Hasan Suroor, 'M.F. Husain, Celebrated Artist, Passes Away in London', *The Hindu*, 9 June 2011.
3. For further discussion, please see M.P. Jain, *Constitutional Law of India*, fifth edition, Wadhwa & Company, New Delhi, 2005.

4. Jonnathan Harris, 'Introduction', in *Globalization and Contemporary Art*, Wiley Blackwell, Sussex, 2011.
5. S. Ananth, Business of Culture in India, CIDASIA, Hyderabad, 2008.
6. 'Saffron Art to Field First Auction of Indian Folk and Tribal Art and Objects, *The Economic Times*, 16 August, 2012.
7. 'How the Arts are Funded Outside the UK', *BBC News*, 20 October, 2010, www.bbcnews.co.uk
8. Shubha Mudgal, 'Globalization and India's Performing Arts', *The Hindu*, 31 December, 2011
9. Report on Cultural Mapping of India under UNESCO's Programme on Cultural Industries and Copyright Policies and Partnerships, Indira Gandhi National Centre for the Arts, New Delhi.

Neeraj Tyagi

Neeraj Tyagi is Executive Chef at The Claridges, New Delhi. He is trained by world famous Garibaldi Restaurant in Singapore and on the other, in German cuisine at the Brix (then Grand Hyatt) with Chef Stephan Foucher and German Chefs Bernad and Ulli. He conducted a New Indian and Lucknavi food festival at the Hulhule Airport Hotel in Maldives for a period of 3 weeks. Neeraj has a long string of achievements having done cookery shows on NDTV and ZEE TV, winning various medals in Culinary contests, both in New Delhi and Mumbai.

11

Global Flavours in the Culinary World

Neeraj Tyagi

Food is the most important ingredient to live and sustain life. The food habits of every individual are culture specific. However, with dynamism being the defining criteria, it is an uncommon practise to find new horizons in food issues also. This paper attempts to understand the food industry, from the, not so well highlighted, the cooking side. These ideas flow from observations of life at various junctures. The paper is divided along three parts, where the first part presents a highlight of Indian economy vis-à-vis food industry, the second part talks about globalization and its implications in realm of food, followed by the concluding note in the third part.

Our food and cuisines have been always affected by the changes in the agriculture and industrial realms.[1] India during the British rule was under sway of several famines, droughts which led to acute paucity of food supply. At that time, cereal grains like unrefined wheat and millets were main items consumed because poverty and hunger were in abundance. In the post-independence era, the Green Revolution led to increase in cereal grain production, which also led to changes in dietary consumption habits towards rice and wheat. The White Revolution by the National Dairy Development Board (NDDB) in the 1970s made become top milk producer and products like milk, cheese added a new flavour for Indian food delicacies and diets.[2] Further, The 'Yellow Revolution' in oilseeds is also to be noted in this regard.

The era of 1990s had carved a new trajectory for our economy. The liberalization of the Indian economy made a big impact on agriculture efforts were made to internationlize it. As the industry grew, there was big demand of grains with better shelf life, there was a new spree for polished and processed grains. Today with new irrigation schemes, introduction of rural credit, incentives to agricultural research with focus on bio-technology frontier and forward linkages such as agro-processing, amongst others has indeed paved way for growth of the cuisine industry in India, which was never thought before.[3]

We are the world's second largest producer of food. Our food processing sector has a wide arena of work from fruits and vegetables to milk products, fisheries, soyabean, and grains, amongst others. However our share in international food trade is dismal.

The cuisine industry has the hallmark of innovation. It is also marked by a certain degree of experimentation as one has to be ready to dabble with taste buds of many. It like preparing things behind a veil, where you do not know what is the nature of the output entity for which it is meant. A cuisine industry professional needs to have a great temperament and passion to make things simple and better every day. This also makes a case for understanding the problematique of global times in various aspects for the culinary delights.

Globalization has become part of everyday vocabulary. Every day we hear the term globalization on the news, read it in the papers, and overhear people talking about it. Globalization signifies a notion of availability, whatever is obtainable is any part of the world can be made accessible in any city. The idea of getting connected also implies sharing and learning from each other. We can learn about customs, ingredients, cooking methods, wines and other important aspect of each city or country.

Changing expectations of the people make us sit and think as how to innovate. The consumer has become more smart and demanding. Keeping in mind the standards have to be improved each day. What earlier was a super service is now considered basic and in order to make yourself better from competition you have to constantly upgrade and make yourself better.

The manpower concerns has changed as well, be it loyalty or any factor regarding the benefits has also rapidly increased. The staff expects fast growth as well as more remuneration each year. The technology has also changed and has been very beneficial for hotels. The surprising fact is the speed of service, where everyone is making an endeavour to make themselves better.

The cuisine industry works with consumers who are wanting to get away from everyday routine, a lunch break or dinner party. It is known for servicing the guests and making sure that their expectations are met. The phenomena of several places to choose from means going above and beyond what they are expecting. It is a global industry. There are many pros and cons in being a globalized organization. It does make doing business a little more difficult. There are cultural, religion, and moral hurdles that have to be jumped over to make sure that the business runs smoothly.

Today the idea of diversity in cuisines is something which we all observe, but we often never stop to think about it. Regional delicacies can be found in every menu, tastes and flavours of different regions know no barriers. There are different restaurants which are based on international cuisine and the success of these restaurant are based on the foreign ingredients which are only available in the foreign markets because of globalization it is possible to procure those ingredients in the local markets.

Further, there is a social divide that one can perceive. At one hand there are cases of hunger & malnutrition in the country. Though there is no exact data on the number of deaths due to malnutrition in the country, but nutritional deficiencies give alarming fears. On the other hand there are issues of substantial fat intake, eating related disorders.[4]

This new age has made us aware about things than ever before. The idea that only a healthy lifestyle is trademark of a working body has become popular. Though our physical body, since ages has been used as a working machine, but now strict diets, slimming procedures, gym culture has had an impact on cuisines as well, therefore we find the demand for heart- healthy food, low sugar, fat free which has also led to rise of building up customised menu for particular health requirements.

Travel has become an inseparable linkage in global urban lives. Today at mere click of a remote control button, we find plethora of choices of where to travel and this has another important bearing for cuisine industry as people have the first thought of being ready to taste on new variety of foods. Further, interest blogs, social media have made people aware about spices, cooking methods of various cuisines than ever before that a Chinese delicacy made in an Indian home can hardly be distinguished from its native land. This has also made us adaptable in our customs than ever before.

Today cities in global era have a marked division of traditional versus contemporary. Food also contains glimpses of that. Let take an example herein the National Capital Territory of Delhi, one gets to have the glimpse of walled city, *samosas, jalebis, parathas*, amongst others can be seen all over to have mouth watering effect but the platter changes in entire spectrum once we move down to the other parts of the main city.

The childhood of current generation must be full of stories about eating at a foreign land and trying out food there. However, in the current times, one can get a taste of the French, Chinese, Italian, Mexican, Mediterranean, Mexican, amongst others in one go. To narrate an example here how the city of Ahmedabad in India known famously for its *dhoklas* now is home to foods from various countries and the enterprising spirit of this city to keep pace with global mindsets has made it all the more successful here.[5] Globalization thus becomes a highly complex notion as cultural homogenization is working along simultaneously along with breeding cultural diversity.

New options are being discovered. In a recent act, the idea

of venture capital aiming for food starts ups to connect demand delivery services from local farms, invent new foods, meat and egg substitutes from plants are being explored.[6]

With the rise in disposable incomes, eating out gives quality time to people together, where they have to spend less time on daily chores like cooking, juxtaposed with the awareness generated by media makes the food industry a good player to face all market odds. Today the business players, looking at this societal feature, often opt for a chain of restaurants in order to diversify their business portfolio. The new opportunities generated by idea of franchises further makes an interesting case with both sides being at a sound level, the foreign player can reduce the overhead costs and the domestic player getting access to new business.

The global era is marked by speed. Food is also not spared here as we witness the rise of the fast food culture with its readymade availability and quick consumption. Just a walk down the lane of any Indian market, one finds the line-up, namely McDonald's, Burger King, Taco Bell, Subway, Kentucky Fried Chicken (KFC). They may have been controversial in their mainland and often been victims of new claims by several ecologists and vegans, yet one cannot gloss over the fact that India has become a new home to them. This impact of global ethos on lives, culture of a common man can be summed up in what can be called as soft power.

Power is not only about capacities to do things but also about capability to cast an influence over others. Great powers in the world are not based on huge armies, military mights or being a giant in politics. The cult of the global world is such that power does not flow from the barrel of the gun. It is decentralised in realms which are close to people, namely food, music, technology amongst others. They cast an influence over our hearts and minds. The attraction shall make one win over coercion.[7]

It is interesting to find as to how the food sector has a huge latent potential to develop. It has further ventured out as a new arena for entertainment where eating out has become a regular feature in our lives. The changing consumption habits of consumers and emergence of new players in the sector are essential to be factored in this growth saga.

India is a leader in food grains, fruits and vegetables, where food processing industry even gave a competition to other sectors like manufacturing. Today we have mega food parks and cold storage facility which has given a new zeal. Unfortunately, there are reports which present stark facts like the food processing industries utilises less than half fund in the allocated plan. The need of the hour is to rectify this deficit.[8]

Today's market condition suggest that one has to be judicious at our expenses which does not means cost cutting, as it may drop down the quality. 'Managing the cost' is the term rather industry specialist use at it means without compromising on quality we control our expense and prioritize the requirement. This enables to sustain during tough months and have consistency in the bottom line throughout the year.

We need to produce more and be prepared when the demand is there and on the other hand control the supply when we do not have the same quantum of business. Change is inevitable and it is the most important aspect of life. However, the silver lining in the cloud is that there are only benefits in change as it gives you more learning and you never know that you create something better than before.

The generations coming ahead needs to have more patience and be the strong advocate of change management. Listening is a very important skill which most of us ignore should be considered very important as it helps you learn for free.

The agrarian sector is seasonal in nature, impacted by monsoons, economic slowdown and mismatch between demand and supply which leads to food inflation. The tax structures in the India's food services industry such as excise and service tax, value added tax add to multicity of structures.[9] Reforms like better tax structure for guests, regulation of excise duties, controlling fluctuating market prices, support of government by providing better infrastructure, amongst others shall go in a long to augur well.

REFERENCES

1. Kamala Krishnaswamy and Ruchi Vaidya, 'Evolving food habits in India', *Food Facts First*, 7 December, 2012.
2. Harvard hails White Revolution, Times New Network, *The Times of India*, 12 March, 2013.
3. Way paved for another Green Revolution, *The Economic Times*, New Delhi, 9 July, 2004.
4. 'Deaths Due to Malnutrition in India', 8 September, 2011, www.indiasanitationportal.org.
5. 'Global flavours now rule Ahmedabad's platter', Times News Network, *Times of India*, 7 February, 2010.
6. 'Venture capitalists in Silicon Valley making big bets on food start-ups', *New York Times*, 30 April, 2013.
7. For further discussion see, Joseph S. Nye Jr., *Soft Power: The Means to Success in World Politics*, New York: Public Affairs Book, 2004
8. 'Food processing industries utilises less than half fund in 11th Plan', Press Trust of India, 22 March, 2013.
9. 'Multiple taxes pose growth barriers for food industry: NRAI', Press Trust of India, New Delhi, 26 April, 2013.

Rachna Sharma

Recently conferred with the prestigious 'leading woman in hospitality' award in the 4th International Women Leadership Summit 2013, Rachna is an expert hospitality professional since a decade. She has held progressive responsibilities in start ups and top sales & marketing leadership roles contributing to successful financial gains and business wins employing positive and ambitious drive. She is currently responsible for strategic development of an international hotel company in India. Rachna is also a philanthropist and is working towards urban women empowerment.

12

Global Context and Challenges for 'Atithi Devo Bhavah'

Rachna Sharma

Introduction

Travel and tourism is the largest service industry globally in terms of gross revenue and foreign exchange earnings. It is also one of the largest employment generators in the world. It has been a major social phenomenon and is driven by social, religious, recreational, knowledge seeking and business interests and motivated by the human urge for new experience, adventure, education, and entertainment. Tourism is both cause and consequence of economic development. It has the potential to stimulate other sectors in the economy owing to cross-synergistic benefits and its backward and forward linkages.

To begin with, the idea that tourism is like octopus, its tentacles reach out to various aspects of our life like coastal development is an apt line to underline the arguments presented here.[1] The start and end point of any tourism idea is the government, for instance national parks to save wildlife, drive boost to economy. It is the government that decides the tourist influx via its policies, exchange rates. It is therefore natural to think of ways this sector has worked at a time when the state and the government are paving out ways for market factors.

One has to also comprehend at the outset, that the hotel industry is contingent on discretionary spending, thus its growth then becomes related to the economic growth.

At the global level, there seems to be a dis-connect between institutions and industry. It is United Nations World Tourism Organization (UNWTO) and World Trade Organization (WTO), as an international treaty, that recognizes travel as an important industry with its multi-facted ramifications. GATS—General Agreement on Goods and Services and European Currency Trades also recognize its significance.

The Indian Hospitality Industry is one of the fastest growing sectors of the Indian economy. Riding on the economic growth and rising income levels that India has been experiencing in the past few years, it has emerged as one of the key sectors driving the country's economy.

However, the observations in this paper are primarily limited to an urban setting. It is assumed that there is need to comprehend the repercussions produced by external factors like tourism, whichever are contingent on other factors namely the parameters of the economy.

Globalization

Globalization is a series of social, economical, technological, cultural, and political changes that have promoted interdependence and growth. It is a historical process that results from human innovation and technological progress

The very strike of the word 'globalization' produces a collage of motley perspectives. For some it conjures up images of electronic communications: an email, global media, popularization of mobile phones for example, for others it is about trade and confluence, and the ability to buy say coca-cola in rural villages in Africa.

Thomas Firedman's idea in the book, *The World is Flat* make us think ourselves as extremely lucky to have the chance to be a part of this unique era in human history. Globalization is a main cause for the convergence that is bringing the nations of the world together more and more every year.

There is a gradual acceptance of a global world with rise in communications and technology which has made us carve out the contours of thinking process as that of a 'global village'. This shall virtually lead to rise of an international global society also. Today change is moving in such a rapid manner that policy makers are also pondering over corrective actions of the policies of the past.

Globalization has multiplied the international intensity of competition. In such realm, a knowledge based economy shall replace the erstwhile Fordist model. This knowledge based economy shall use the skills of the manpower to the core which shall translate into new challenges for human resource management also.

When the reach of government power over certain areas goes out, it moves to the domain of market where we have rise of global firms. These organization do, in fact, benefit the world, because it brings together multiple ideas and combines them to form a common idea. Many of the world's problems are solved through world organizations, because a group of collaborated countries come together and organize solutions to problems that plague the world.

The global era needs to be distinguished from its intensity and scope. Global firms would seek to cater to the interest of the dominant shareholders. Developing countries may find them at an unequal position with respect to the developed ones. The need of the hour is to deliberate over the course of actions taken and induce corrective measures, which this paper shall try to enshrine.

From the perspective of a practitioner of the hospitality industry, globalization would signify parameters like what J. Scholte would hold—internationalization, westernization, de-territorilization, interconnectedness and universalization. What is important to note is that various aspects of globalization are co-related, that is, if economic globalization has made economies integrated, then it has fuelled new discoveries and innovations in technological realm, which has further led to a certain degree of homogenization of culture and social life, leading to a larger societal impact of the global being perceived as percolated towards the local.

When we analyse hospitality, at an individual level it involves diverse range of population, at the industry level it is multi-faceted, and at cultural level it involves several disciplines.

Indian Scenario

The Indian hospitality industry has grown significantly over the last ten years. This growth can be attributed to variety of factors like societal factors, consumer trends, more disposable incomes and exposure to more and more options. It has witnessed a very strong growth both in terms of numbers and new concepts.

Seen from a legal constitutional approach, Tourism and Hospitality are a state subject in the Constitution of India. Police, law and order are State subjects as per the Seventh Schedule of the Constitution of India. Therefore, prevention of crime against tourists/foreign tourists is primarily the responsibility of the State Governments/Union Territory (UT) Administrations.

An industry needs a spurt from the society for its growth and development. The rise of the middle class with higher disposable incomes, easy availability of credit narrated the saga of increase in affordability and a certain degree of preference for travel which drove the growth in the travel, tourism and hospitality industries in the country.

From a time when it was seen as one of not so significant a sector, realising the potential of the industry to let nation bandwagon on its soft power, the government has now allowed for 100 per cent FDI in the hotel industry which includes construction of hotels, resorts, and recreational facilities through the automatic route. Further, the sector has been in tandem with the growth in other sectors like health. An instance here could be the commencement of 'Medical Visa' for tourists coming for treatment.

Tourism has also been pivotal in foreign affairs, as we can see in the provision of visa-on-arrival for tourists from select countries which includes countries like Japan, New Zealand, Finland; amongst others. Elimination of customs duty for import of raw materials, alcohol, capital subsidy programme for budget hotels, exemption of Fringe Benefit Tax on crèches, employee sports, and guest house facilities are further incentives introduced by the state keeping in mind the potential of this sector in today's liberal era. With further opening up of civil aviation, it has spelled boom for the hospitality industry in attracting foreign players.[2]

Further, India is out pricing itself as a holiday destination over other competing destinations like China, Brazil and South Africa which have followed a much better approach of gradual increase in tariff with parallel growth in quality of product and services. By strengthening regional business ties, South and South-East of Asia witnessed strong intra-regional demand. Uniformity in price points across various seasons and a competitive pricing against the South East Asian destinations will definitely help in getting more tourist arrivals in the country in the long run.

International tourist arrivals rose from 682 million in 2001 to 920 million in 2008. The global travel and tourism industry experienced a downturn in 2009 due to the global economic and financial meltdown. The industry was affected by low business volumes and consumer confidence, given the uncertainty about factors such as availability of credit, exchange rates, employment, and the H1N1 virus. Consequently, tourist arrivals fell worldwide in 2009. Nevertheless, tourist arrivals increased in the last quarter of 2012, led by the recovery in the Asia Pacific and the Middle East.

Over the past few years, the global economy has been affected by various natural, social and economic headwinds; the earthquake in Japan during March-2011, floods in Thailand in 2011, civil unrest in the Arab countries, economic crisis in the EU. Despite these upheavals, foreign tourist arrivals (FTA) to India has grown.

Gone are those days when the mere name of a hotel was a guiding instinct. This has made the hotel industry also to diversify its marketing strategies away from realm of numbers by factoring in the social milieu *vis-à-vis* blogs, networking sites, travel sites to nurture choice and provide information.

Land is a scared scarce asset. With the real estate prices shooting to unimaginable levels, the task of maintaining a hotel is herculean. This has made the hotel players to venture out away from the metro cities towards emergent cities like Hyderabad, Pune, Jaipur, amongst others.

Global times have often made people much more sophisticated in terms of preferences. Rise of micro markets in primary cities, liking to stay near place of work are certain factors that have propelled hotel company's to set up diverse locations within a city.

A lot of action is happening in India in Tier II and III cities and the industry has evolved quite a bit. With international brands entering India, creating more employment opportunities, bringing price parity and thus generating more demand, industry has seen remarkable growth in the domestic tourism which was very minimal before. One has to also point out that today the idea of choice is a chimera. Choice is a mechanism to get goods and services at prices affordable to them. The idea of a 'brand' within the hotel industry helps to cater to this diversity.[3]

What is remarkable here is that the paraphernalia of a global world, quests for larger markets and profits exist within a highly fragmented and labour intensive industry which gives job opportunities and employment to skilled, semi-skilled, and unskilled labour.

The Crossroads: Problematizing 'Atithi Devo Bhava'

The Sanskrit verse of 'Atithi Devo Bhavah' synonymn for the idea that 'the guest is God' has now to deal with several issues in its quest to cater to its notion of hospitality at its best. The global growth perspective is indeed bright for India. When other economies are growing around 2 per cent, the Asian economies are growing at 5-6 per cent. Though India is yet to become a mature economy on lines of the U.S. and Europe, and with China has always having abundant supply aspect, yet we are slightly good from the vantage point of growth.

Today, we have estimated 28,000 branded hotel rooms with our current share of global inbound tourists of 0.6 per cent. This figure is expected to rise to 1 per cent in near times. Now here we are in position of scale in prospective demands but in less supply. One has to bring to light that in a recent move the government found shortage of branded hotel rooms in the country as an acute and further estimated an additional need of 1,80,000 branded hotel rooms. Therefore, the hospitality market in India will witness a new spree in terms of more new players, which is expected to hover around 300 branded hotels attracting an investment of $200 billion in next three years from now.[4] There are claims by several global hotel majors like Marriott, Accor, Hilton, Starwood, Best Western and Carlson to increase their portfolio of hotels by 2015/20, yet what needs to be watched out is that this may reflect the broad intent and may undergo significant changes before actually being finalized keeping mind the new challenges of the global times.

There is also the problem of the imbalance between forces of demand & supply which scaled the average daily Room rate (ADR) to great heights. This factor, along with the exorbitant high tax structure, placed the country to be an expensive tourist destination. Though the business travel was limited to key metro cities, the leisure destinations and Meetings-Incentives-Conference-Exhibitions (MICE) business got effected to a large extent.

In an era when global issues have a local impact and ramifications, hospitality also faces the challenge of the sustainability criteria. There have been efforts done to chalk out indicators for the accommodation sector, including hotels and resorts, which has been taken for consideration as part of drawing up such norms for tourism in the country as a whole.

In India, the hotel industry can boast of having around 1,30,000 classified and 2.5 million unclassified rooms, which also makes it as one of the biggest energy consumers in the country. In the present state, there are no yardsticks put around cutting energy consumption and their carbon footprint.

Issues of climate change, global warming and rise in temperatures put forward an uncanny question before our hotel industry which is growing annually at good pace, but unfortunately will also add to the malaise of increase in emissions. The government is contemplating efforts to make hotels stand up to the sustainability criteria which is pegged as a voluntary scheme with incentives to those who adhere.[5] The pressing question is the need to balance out competition, quest for diversification and quality of the brand with the new macro agenda. Sustainability in the workplace will be key as this is how a company's image will be seen in an ever increasing view of the current climate changes and their impact. To add more, the problems of today has also made the sector to search for innovative solutions, like it has brought into prominence the concept of eco-tourism and agri-tourism.

India's consumer market is in a state of change. Today's consumer needs constant change and new products because they have a very short attention span, triggered by the remote control culture. Vacations have emerged as the top priority for disposing extra money. In the hospitality sector, the story is no different, with the guests today becoming increasingly unpredictable. This also has an impact on the efficacy of many loyalty programmes which hotels target towards their customers.

Today service apartments, time sharing, fractional ownership and company hotels or guest houses, have immense potential to grow. Diversification is being seen as the key to survival in the long run, to mention here how SPAs are appearing at hotel properties at a remarkable rate & are becoming independent profit centres. Even the corporate sector and real estate sector are being lured by the wellness agenda. The new millennium has made spa industry as a melting point for range of products that enhance good life as a successor to the strains generated by the global dynamic lives we live in.[6] To add to that, cafes, lounges & bars, which have high profit margins, are increasingly mushrooming in various hotels across India.

Tourism and hospitality is not a clear cut sector yet its importance can be seen from the fact that it embraces all aspects of national life. As held by MacCannel, it is an ideological reframing of the History and has the power to re-shape cultures. Cultural differences do play an important role for any tourist destination, yet amidst all this the silver lining in the cloud is rise of transcendental global standards and practices. The features of quality, multiple players, role of public authorities, corporate price structure will always be important in shaping the industry in global era. The need of the hour is to factor in the pressures generated by the localization aspect by questioning anti-cartel, anti-monopoly laws.[7]

The European debt crisis and turbulence in the macro economic outlook made the global consumer sentiment as anxious and conservative and cost cutting efforts have been introduced in view of weak corporate results. During the economic down cycle, the faster pace of deceleration in the hotels industry. A strong underlying economy then becomes an imperative for sustained recovery.

Besides taxation and other macro-economic issues, there are human resource related issues which are needed to add a spree to this sector. The most crucial hunt in the times to come will be for right talent and manpower. Business success is driven by having the right people to deliver the strategy and create growth. The new generation will continue to look for employers who embrace their desire for challenging work, amazing development and training opportunities, and travel possibilities. Employers need to recognise that young joiners today and in the future will have different demands and aspirations to those generations that have preceded us. One has also to mention here that bright and educated younger generation has never considered hotel industry as a progressive employment option. That has to be changed by more lucrative compensations and development plans.

Technology will be at the centre of everything we do, in ways that may now be unimaginable. All peripherals used now would probably no longer be used in the future. Everyone has to keep up the pace with the change in modern technology.

Shortage of skilled manpower in the hotel industry will be a big challenge to cater to. There are 51 institutes which are recognised by the National Council for Hotel Management and Catering Technology (NCHMCT), a body associated with the tourism ministry. However, this is inadequate in relation to the needs of the times.[8] To talk of augmenting the capacity further brings forward other issues like compensation, infrastructure, and viability, amongst others. If this scenario will persist, it shall mop up the profits for the industry, with the costs of already existing employees to scale up with additional spending on in-house training programs.

An important pause needed in this deliberation of global times is that while we talk about rise in government expenditure, flourishing economy, new strategies, a word of some social security for those who have worked in the industry for years with no pensions to fall back on when the external beauty and enthusiasm deceives them with rise in age. Though there are proposals for formation of Tourist Security Organization, yet this largely is confined to the state sector and excludes the private sector.[9] Further, we may talk about moving back of state, we need to ensure due security measures and certain social ethos for respect for foreign travellers.

In a nutshell, the way for the future lies in adapting to global best practices with an attempt to make it work in the indigenous realm with an all-encompassing vision for industry. A certain gradation of our responsibility towards society should dominate the larger corporate world wide interconnected agenda with concerns about demographic changes, climate and sustainability becoming the main business drivers. Seen from a holistic perspective, hospitality & tourism shall be the most dynamic catalyst for ever-changing tomorrow's lifestyle

REFERENCES

1. Elizabeth Beckar, *Overbooked: The Exploding Business of Travel and Tourism*, New York: Simon & Schuster, 2013.
2. 'Hospitality sector attracts $3.2 bn FDI in Apr-Feb FY13', Press Trust of India, New Delhi, 5 May 2013
3. Tim Knowles, Dimitrios Diamantris and J. Mourhabi, *Globalization of Tourism and Hospitality*, London: Thomson Learning, 2006.
4. 'Hospitality Sector to Attract over $200 Bn in Next 3 Years: Report', *Live Mint*, 2 April 2013, New Delhi.
5. Moulishree Srivastava, 'New Norms may Provide a Push for Hospitality Sector', *Live Mint*, 25 May 2012
6. Marc Cohen and Gerard Bodekar, *Understanding Global Spa Industry*, Oxford, UK: Elsevier, 2008.
7. For further discussions see, Chris Cooper and Sarah Wahab, *Tourism in Age of Globalization*, New York: Routledge, 2001.
8. 'Skill Shortage Threat to Hotel Industry Growth', *Live Mint*, New Delhi, 7 October 2012
9. 'Planning Commission allots Rs. 1282 crore for Tourism', New Delhi, 26 April 2013, www.Indiahospitalityreview.com

Dr. Abhimanyu Singh Arha

Dr. Abhimanyu Singh Arha is a historian serving as an Assistant Professor at the Department of History, Maharaja Ganga Singh University, Bikaner, Rajasthan. Belonging to the desert town of Jodhpur, he is an alumni of St. Stephen's College, Delhi and a PhD from Jawaharlal Nehru University, New Delhi. He began his career as a guest faculty at his alma mater, St. Stephen's College. His area of research includes : medieval history, history of ecology, the Thar desert and its changing profile, Rajasthani language and the philosophy of History. An advocate of respecting the delicate bond between ecology and its inhabitants, the author is a regular blogger and a poet.

13

Globalization, Cultural Heritage and Travel Industry

Scope of Developing New Tourist Attractions

Dr. Abhimanyu Singh Arha

Introduction

This article is an attempt to delineate the impact of globalization on the local population and culture and their reciprocal influence in order to advocate for the development of such tourist destinations which have hitherto been side-lined. In an age of enhanced cross-cultural mobility and interaction, tourism is one industry which has offered a deep insight into the various debates and contentions that revolve around globalization, its trends and its impact. The author presents a grass-root level analysis and discussion over the core issues as conspicuous developments, events, challenges and changes have been observed over a period of time in an area that attracts a sizeable tourist population per annum.

Rajasthan: New Avenues in Tourism Industry

The charm of history, rural traditions preserved intact, beautiful landscapes marked by breathtaking view of lakes and sand-dunes and royal hospitality has enabled this state to emerge as one of the leading holiday destinations for international as well as domestic tourists[1].

It is interesting to see that media and commercialization have promoted certain select destinations only while simultaneously pushing a few, historically famous destinations into oblivion. Places such as Mount Abu[2] and Bikaner, which were one of the most favorite holiday destinations of Britishers and other Europeans residing in India during the nineteenth and twentieth century, have now come to occupy peripheral positions along the busy tourist circuits. During the days of Raj, these two destinations were highly important dates on the annual holiday calendars of *sahibs* and *memsaabs*. Mount Abu was dubbed as the 'Kashmir of Rajputana'. It lay close to the important highway connecting Delhi, the then imperial capital to the rich port province of Gujarat. Located atop the highest peaks of the majestic Aravalli ranges, the hill station (one of its kind in the entire state of Rajasthan) offered serene climate and lush green environs. It was a hotspot for bio-diversity as in those days of pristine environment, the forests surrounding the mountains were home to tigers, leopards, Indian bear and many other exotic species of wild animals. If we take into account oral narrations, as a source of history, we learn from the accounts of old people residing at Abu that in the early twentieth century, during the winter season, the famous Nakki lake, situated in the centre of the hill station, would freeze, thus becoming an excellent venue for ice-skating frivolity.

Likewise, Bikaner was the ultimate holiday spot for royal dignitaries from London and eminent aristocrats of the British Empire coming from all over the world. The state of Bikaner was one of the premier states of Rajputana and its monarchs took active interest in evoking strong paternal affection from the British paramountcy. Maharaja Ganga Singh who rose to prominence at the royal court of London due to his honourable and dutiful services to the crown surpassed all his contemporary Maharajas in fomenting special ties with British ruling elite. He was the Hon. ADC to HRH The Prince of Wales in 1902, later serving him when he became His Majesty King George V, the King-Emperor, in 1910. In addition to being a member of the Central Recruiting Board-India in 1917, he represented India at the Imperial War Conference held in AD 1917, the Imperial War Cabinet and the Paris Peace Conference of 1919. Ganga Singh ji was Chancellor of the Indian Chamber of Princes from 1920-26 and also represented India as a delegate at the fifth session of the League of Nations in 1924. Consequently, many British officials started frequenting Bikaner where they were showered upon with princely hospitality and offered unique thrills. Over a period of time, invitations for winter hunting sprees at the heart of this desert kingdom became one of the most glamorous and sought after social events of the elite in British India.

The winter shooting season, attracting big-wigs of the Raj, promised huge catch of the rare Great Indian Bustard and other exotic bird species. The guests were lodged at the grand and majestic Gajner lake palace, a beautiful palace built besides a desert lake resembling an oasis. Guests would include top-brass aristocrats, bureaucrats and other members of Indian royalty. A long list of Viceroys visited this marvel of tourism including Lord Curzon, Lord Linlithgow, Lord Irwin and Lord Mountbatten. One of the greatest honours for Maharaja Ganga Singh was the grand event when the Emperor of India King George V and Queen Mary visited Bikaner in AD 1911 when they embarked upon a journey to India in order to grace the grand Delhi Durbar[3]. Much of all this is lost today and Jaisalmer has overtaken this 'jewel of the Thar' as the penultimate holiday spot for the authentic Thar experience. Global media coverage and projection of a select destination (as in this cae, Jaisalmer) results in a shift of business opportunities and industry-growth. Thus, on the geopolitical level, global media has made a significant contribution, as major mediators of tourism experience of any destination. It has invariably led to the making or breaking of a particular location in the International tourist circuit depending on the leverage it provides or does not provide.

The tourism industry suddenly saw a rise in Jaisalmer during the 1970's and within a span of two decades, it reached a 'take-off' phase. There was a splurge in hotels with some big names joining the fray. The real advantage of booming hotel industry was reaped by the nearby metropolis Jodhpur, the only big city in proximity that offered air connectivity. Jaisalmer soon caught the imagination of the increasingly globalized globetrotting traveller's community and assumed an important position on the world tourist map. This story of an upsurge, however, was accompanied by some profound disadvantages as well. Several reports and studies have come to establish the rise in the use of drugs and incidences of AIDS among the indigenous population catering to this industry. Illegal hunting and littering have caused serious concerns for the all ready fragile desert ecology. Apart from these evil effects, another serious depravity that has set in is the irretrievable damage caused to authentic indigenous culture by the avaricious commercial packaging. Komal Kothari, a renowned folklorist and ethnomusicologist, has pointed out that local music performers have discarded many traditional musical instruments and have been producing showy musicals garnished with Hindi cinema music. This leads to destruction of the distinctive musical ethnicity of the region which is one of the main incentives for people coming from far-off countries. It gets replaced with a crass art form which is detrimental for future growth[4].

Thus, it has been pointed out that lop sided growth of tourism sector necessitates active and potent corrections and interventions at the policy level. The need of the hour is to originate strong institutions which would design, develop and apply sound policies in this sector. Some scholars have pointed out that 'theoretical thinking in tourism and actual tourism policies are still somewhat behind the times'[5]. Alarms are being raised at the manner in which tourism sector is being handled at the international level. While the main agents of tourism—airlines, hotel chains, tour operators, tourism administrators etc. defend Globalization, adequate steps are not taken to critically analyse its content and implications. Carefully delineated tourism policy-international as well as national, should be put into action. A great deal of vacillation accrues out of the tendency to blame inaction on the notion that much of this sector's growth is guided by the uninhibited play of market forces.

One of the corner-stones of a solid tourism policy in the wake of recent trends of Globalization and the longing for a true 'glocal' experience is diversification of tourism supply. This step entails meticulously launching new products and destinations. Traveler's priorities have to be understood comprehensively in order to ascertain the saleability or marketability of the new products or destinations to be developed. What a traveler wants and expects from his trip is something which should be researched in depth and then worked upon. A tourist's anticipation should be taken into account. Only when the marketing strategy of a new product would be convincing enough as well as attractive enough, will a sizeable share of annual traffic be diverted to the new location. A great variety of competitive tour options is one of the results of increasing Globalization which has been felt in this particular segment of Indian tourism i.e. Rajasthan also. Hence, an effective and lucrative tourism policy should tackle the issue of projection of new destinations as well.

The target of popularising a select segment of a vast travel encounter can be achieved only by a holistic development of that location along with its surrounding attractions and possibilities. Leiper's concept of tourism types need to be employed here for a better formulation of directives[6]. There are many facets of Bikaner which can enhance the tourism potential of entire northern Rajasthan. However, considerable efforts have to be made in polishing and presenting these facets sophisticatedly. According to Leiper, while planning a holiday, a traveler is not drawn towards a destination only because of a single object—a church, castle or a cemetery. Rather, it is a combination of several social conditions and 'markers' that cause people to visit that place as a means to fulfilling a want or desire. Thus, 'attraction' is more about the whole package than merely the nucleus. Markers here refers to information sources about the nuclear elements of the attraction. He argues that markers link the humans with nuclear elements of the attraction. Basic infrastructure of information, information sources and information dissemination needs to be strengthened.

The question of utmost importance that is being raised at this point of the discourse is that what peculiarities of the target destination can be highlighted? As mentioned earlier, Rajasthan draws a large proportion of the tourist crowd coming to India. The domestic tourist also visits select locations only as the travel itineraries are, more or less, fixed due to high levels of competition leaving no space for experimenting with new options. This makes it all the more challenging to accommodate a new destination within the oft-beat tourist track. The answer lies in striking a middle path between natural as well as cultural heritage of Bikaner.

The author has been fortunate enough to traverse much of the length and breadth of the Bikaner sub-division- comprising of four districts of Rajasthan, namely, Bikaner, Sri Ganganagar, Hanumangarh and Churu on official duties, field visits and educational tours. On the basis of personal experience and discussions with academicians, scientists, administrators, investors and hoteliers, we arrived at the conclusion that immense tourism potential lies in store for this 'poem out of the Thar'; provided development enthusiasts are as convinced as we may want them to be. The advantages of Globalization are an asset in this case as it equips them with all the necessary machinery and tools to effectively implement ambitious stratagems.

To begin with, Bikaner offers the unique opportunity to strike a healthy and beneficial balance between natural as well as cultural heritage. Speaking of the natural heritage in the form of landscape, ecology and nature, this location exhibits immense beauty and pleasure. The most exotic picture of this land which, if marketed well, can transform this quiet, serene and charming 'frontier-land' into a paradise for those seeking solace in the sands, is the picture of the grand Indira Gandhi Canal meandering its way from north-east to south-west through the Thar desert. One of the world's largest irrigation project, this canal has transformed the lives of the people of this desert region by a huge margin and if this could be captured by tourism promoters, then there is no doubt about the rich revenues that this attraction would generate. There are a few spots along the bends and turns of this mighty man-made river which are marked with tall, undulating sand-dunes. Imagine a well-maintained resort offering regal tented accommodation atop such a lofty dune with a commanding view of far-off knuckle-head dune formations. In addition to this natural bounty, in terms of tourist attraction, are the range of lakes and oasis strewn around the landscape- e.g. Gajner lake (holding an added incentive of a grand lake palace), Darbari lake (a former hunting ground), Tal Chappar (a well-stocked wild-life reserve) and Kolayat (an ancient pilgrimage center as captivating and intriguing as its more renowned cousin—the Pushkar lake near Ajmer).

It is through the realm of ecology and nature that we can construe a peculiar cultural heritage of Bikaner and highlight its enigma. The history that surrounds this desert kingdom is a tale of constant negotiations and re-negotiations of its people with the harsh climate around. Rao Bika, the eldest son of Rao Jodha, carved out this principality in the fifteenth century AD by the valorous exploits of his warrior clan. This engaging story contains pictographic accounts of how the desert was tamed which presents the refined tourists with enriching experience. Secondly, unlike Jaisalmer, Bikaner had been one of the premier states of Rajputana and hence, one can see remnants of that glory in every nook and corner of he town. Talking about the medieval times, the Junagarh fort displays the rich syncretic culture of the Rajputs and the Mughals whereas the nineteenth and twentieth century monuments show how monarchies were striving hard to modernise their kingdoms with introduction of educational institutions, electricity, hospitals and the railways. Coming to the present age, one can have a rendezvous with history and culture in the streets of this dusty town. Located in the heart of this city is the state headquarters of the Rajasthan State Archives, a mine of historical information containing thousands of manuscripts, inscriptions, rare publications and reports of the Raj and photographs from yester years. Finally, if one embarks upon a 'heritage walk' through the old fortified town, one witnesses ornate buildings called havelis carved out of colourful stone and a hustly-bustly world beaming with life and vigour around these structures. One can also acquaint oneself with the social spaces of interaction among the indigenous people if the visit is timed during a lazy afternoon or a cool summer night when people stay awake till late at night only to chitter-chatter while perched on *balcao* like styled small verandahs of their little homes. It is only through the ramifications of the recent waves of Globalization that our awareness regarding the true intrinsic value of such cultural fortune has been augmented. It should be one of the imperatives of a culturally vibrant state and society to savour such wealth and invest in its future to generate more wealth and opportunities. As Dallen Timothy maintains, the task of preserving the local heritage and culture assumes a position of significance in the face of a continuous rise in the global demand for varying cultural experiences in the tourism industry[7].

Conclusion

It is an incontestable fact that Globalization, as an irreversible trend, has contributed to the expansion of the tourism industry like never before. However, it is highly opportune at the moment on the part of policy-makers and managers to innovate and develop alternative channels of traffic in order to generate more revenue from this industry. In a country like ours which is culturally rich and vibrant, such an endeavour is facilitated by sheer magnetism of age-old antiquity and varied cultural hues lying hidden in very many locations strewn across the length and breadth of the sub-continent. The above discourse shows how Bikaner has immense potential of emerging as a tourist hot-spot along the Delhi-Jaipur-Jaisalmer route, the last one being the most exotic travel destination in remote Thar desert. Bikaner's proximity to Jaisalmer can be leveraged to show-case the former as an added tourist attraction in the world-famous Rajasthan circuit. The task of tapping such a reserved potential becomes achievable due to the opportunities and abilities provided by the prospects of growing Globalization. Targetted advertisements and innovative strategizing can enable projecting this wonderful desert city and its environs as a unique travel experience and consequently, Bikaner can occupy an important position on the world tourist map, a position it once enjoyed in its heyday.

REFERENCES

1. In the year 2000, the number of foreign tourists visiting Rajasthan was 6,23,100 which accounted for 23.52% of the total foreign tourist arrivals in India. The number of domestic tourist arrivals was 73,74,391 placing the state on eight rank in terms of number of tourist arrivals state-wise.
   State of Environment Report for Rajasthan: 2007, pp. 108-09. http://210.212.96.131, 19.05.2013.
2. Henderson, Carol E. and Veisgrau, Maxine K. ed., *Raj Rhapsodies: Tourism, Heritage and the seduction of History*, Ashgate Publishing Ltd., Hampshire, 2007.
3. Rathore, L.S., *Regal Patriot: Maharaja Ganga Singh of Bikaner*, Roli Books, New Delhi, 2007.
4. Menon, A.G. Krishna, *Case Study of the Effects on Tourism on Culture and Environment*, UNESCO, Bangkok, 1993, pp. 15-28. http://unesdoc.unesco.org.
5. Fayos-Sola, E. and Bueno, A. P., "Globalization, national tourism policy and International Organizations" in Sarah Wahab and Chris Cooper ed., *Tourism in the Age of Globalization*, Routledge, London, 2001, p. 45.
6. Leiper, N. "Tourist attraction systems". *Annals of Tourism Research,* 17(3), 1990, pp. 367-384.
7. Timothy, Dallen J., *Cultural Heritage and Tourism: An Introduction,* Channelview Publications, Bristol, 2011, p. 78.

Cyriac Kodath

Cyriac Kodath is a Graduate in Economic Honors from St Stephens College in New Delhi and a Post Graduate in Development Studies with a specialization in Public Policy and Management from the Institute of Social Studies, The Hague, Netherlands. He has worked for Tsunami Rehabilitation Projects and coastal development initiatives implemented in fishing community settlements for 4 years with Environmental NGOs in Tamil Nadu. His research interests include Environmental Policy Analysis and Design, Public Sector Audits and Rational Assessment of the Political Decision Making Process. The views that he presents here are from his experience of witnessing the latent underlining of the development politics of global era.

14

A Crisis of Politics and Development Satisficing: Flirting with Disaster in Vizhinjam

Cyriac Kodath

> *Satisficing – An act of moving satisfactorily to the next, required point of least change. Often used in Policy Paralysis.*

Development Policy is often confused with Political Agenda. In Kerala the politics of development far exceeds its share of importance in comparison with actual developments. Political leadership is synonymous with leaders, visionaries, planners and policy decision makers. Inherent systemic inefficiency and corruption is the perceived explanation for development gains lost in translation during the implementation of public projects. In the context of today, development intervention is past urgency. Considering simply the Growth of Indian per capita GDP over the past decade and the corresponding increase in absolute numbers of extent of poverty, the results are striking to highlight the complete failure of the trickle down theory as a function of merely GDP Growth in India. To some extent, the failure is to be blamed on corruption, inefficiency and negligence in ethical governance. However, it cannot be escaped that the root blame for these symptoms is the disappropriate and often overwhelming political development agenda that consumes the minds of policy makers and public debate.

Today in the case of Kerala, a spectacular case of misguided and misplaced priorities exist as part of the main stream political agenda for development and economic growth. South of the capital city of Trivandrum, the Fishing Villages of Vizhinjam, Adimalathura and Poovar are being risked permanently in the name of supposed development. The southernmost stretch of coastline in Kerala, from the Vizhinjam Fishing Harbour and southwards into Tamil Nadu, is a 15 km stretch of untouched virgin coastline that is home to over 10 Lakh Fishermen including the residents of the Vizhinjam Fishing Harbour. The current plan for a container transshipment terminal is actually, according to media reports and information in the public domain, more than 20 years old. The manifesto of our governance organization and development planning has led to an old and possibly no longer a suitable idea which, gains much prominence and consume publics resources. The overwhelming support at the highest levels of elected government signifies the high political stakes invested into this project. The execution of these large development projects in Kerala has been very often difficult and a constant process of slow lethargically delayed implementation. Several cases of Metro Rails, Smart Cities, Waste Management, Electricity Infrastructure, Pollution of Water Bodies, Health, Education, Public Distribution System and Loss of Biodiversity, to name a few, are examples of plans gone wrong. A visible gap exists between plans and what is finally implemented.

The need for a Transshipment Terminal Container Port which, for all practical purposes, is a storage warehouse for large container ships next to the water and is questionable in the context of Kerala's economy, the overall global economic scenario and current market dynamics of the shipping industry in this region. Though ship access to Vizhinjam is present but significantly better alternatives exist in Cochin, Tuticorin and Colombo. These issues along with a sizable debt burden that the State of Kerala would need to bear in order to finance the port is a classical situation of political Russian roulette with the public exchequer. All levels of politicians follow the blind support as a consequence of the propaganda from the top leadership. The Vizhinjam Port project has already been universally accepted by all political parties as the next big development project in Kerala and is a front runner for debate and for scoring election points. The public and economic rationale of the Vizhinjam Port was never required to be established as a result of the political propaganda highlighting the port as a top priority all these years.

A policy subversion occurs when due diligence is over taken by political rationale. The idea was not actually for a Port that could boost trade in the southern tip of Kerala, but that of a port in Vizhinjam alone to fulfill the stated objectives. The basis of the notion has an inclination that suggests that the idea for a port in Vizhinjam rose, in as much probability as an easy proclamation, to address the need for Vizhinjam to develop and the failures associated with the efforts needed for inclusive social development in Vizhinjam.

The port itself remained only election speech talk for the first ten years or so since it was recorded that such a plan existed. In 2004, however, the first official act came up with the creation of a special purpose vehicle, VISL, wholly owned by the Government of Kerala. This new entity created by Government Order, appointed with executive powers, consumed State finances, resources and personnel. A princely sum of 400 Crores had been spent in pursuit of the idea to develop a port in the southern tip of Kerala. Entrusted with the task of constructing a Container Transshipment Terminal port, the process of project development falls under the purview of Environmental Impact Assessment Notification 2006 from the Ministry of Environment and Forests. In terms of EIA Guidelines and MOEF Office Memorandums a significant deviation from approved policy existed wherein such Category A—High Environmental Impact Projects ought to be subjected to a scientific process of site selection and environmental scoping. A lapse in performance quality existed for various consultants engaged in the port advisory and technical support. Although since Vizhinjam, as a location and the basis of the very concept for development of the project, was inherently linked to the development of the port, it is likely that consultants were appointed with the understanding to ensure that Vizhinjam remained the site for the port project.

Vizhinjam is a densely populated fishing village that revolves around the operations of the existing harbour that was constructed in 1962 but yet to be commissioned even today. The population survives on abject conditions of polluted ground water, slum housing, vector disease threats, open sewerage drains and almost nil supply of clean drinking water. The low income fishing community finds support within religious institutions more prominently than under government schemes. Christianity, Islam and Hindu religions are present in Vizhinjam. The existence of all fishermen are challenged as a consequence of poor public infrastructure within the Fishing Harbour and in the surrounding habitations. Thousands of low income fishermen sleep in the open harbour areas daily without a shelter over their heads, exposed to pests, rain and rodents. The basic amenities for the fishing community is nonexistent with the women frequenting a small stretch of beach in the north side of the harbour in the absence of toilets, while the men use the beach on the south end of the breakwater. The immense risk for infection through fecal matter infection especially for children who frequent the water within the harbor itself for their ablutions are in stark contrast to what is actually needed and what is finally put forth as the solution for these social development problems.

The Environmental baseline of Vizhinjam is critical on two separate counts. The human baseline, due to the living environment being so challenged and lack of basic infrastructure of water, shelter and electricity contributing to the challenge on one hand is a reality for the residents but when the marine environment is put to risk and challenged, the very income opportunity for this marginalized community is threatened. The Fishery Resource, which is the source of livelihood for the one million plus fishermen in the southern district if subjected to manmade harm, will cause a social crisis of a nature that the State Government does not fully comprehend. The very nature of the political discourse and governance agenda is engineered to overlook this point in the blind pursuit of the planning of the port. The existence of traditional and close shore fishing activities along the Vizhinjam to Poovar coastline is inherent in the social organization with almost all fishermen involved in close shore fishing during times of the year. The capability of the very same government machinery attempting to build the port is vastly inadequate if governance mechanisms in Vizhinjam are called to undertake a clean up effort or disaster management exercise as a consequence of operational or construction impacts and accidents from the port. One can imagine the extent of social and environmental disruption that would eventually occur for the fishing community as a result of something as statistically certain as an oil spill in a port where container ships are planned to frequent. Substantial evidence from the field begs open a rethink of crucial social and environmental aspects of such a port proposed deep within the heart of the Vizhinjam fishing community and threatening their very existence by endangering their source of livelihood and the sustainability of the marine fishery resources.

Additionally the Coastline of Vizhinjam is spectacular. The area is home to one of the most picturesque landscapes with sunsets truly befitting the title as Gods' Own Country. Kerala Tourism Department estimates that total earnings for the State from Tourism presently amounts to 20,000 crores per year. Within the statistics, the average daily expenditure for the foreign tourist is significantly more that Indian tourists. The average duration of stay for foreign travelers is also substantially more than Indians. Foreign tourists started visiting the first and still most prominent beach destination in Kerala, Kovalam Beach which lies just 1 km from the Vizhinjam Fishing Harbour. Worldwide fame on beach tourism in Kovalam, Vizhinjam and Poovar is a well established brand developed through public expenditure and resources. Tourism in Kerala has withstood the economic recession fairly well and growing now for more that 20 per cent for some years. Tourism is also an industry that is highly competitive and based on natural resources being undisturbed. The belt of Kovalam, Vizhinjam and Poovar, that is significant for Tourism, supports over One Lakh, souls directly and indirectly. The concept of beach tourism has evolved in the last 2 decades of tourism in Kerala open to the European and Foreign travellers. Over time resorts in the area and the tourism sector has grown into offering one of India's and Kerala's unique selling point to visitors—Ayurveda Health Tourism. The unique beauty of the coastline and local knowledge of Ayurveda in Kerala has helped develop the tourism sector in Vizhinjam into that where a sizable number of rooms and resorts exist wholly interlinked to an Ayurvedic holiday tourism wherein natural ambience is vital. The key reason for longer stays in the area, as opposed to short stay travellers, are the Ayurveda Massage, Therapy, Diet, Yoga and Meditation that attracts longer stay tourists. A wholesome healing package with a controlled diet results in a visible improvement in health that truly makes visitors to the Ayurveda resorts come back regularly.

All stakeholders in the Tourism Sector will attest that the impact on beaches, once permanently destroying the natural ambience, and coastline will make what Kerala Tourism is known for, lose its single most necessary condition for existence. If the natural beauty and ambience of the area is commercialized and industrialized, the impact will be very severe for the tourism sector in the region. The occurrence and impact on tourism is vastly significant for 2 reasons, the tourism sector provides income and livelihood for several thousand persons and small businesses. It also earns foreign exchange and promotes entrepreneurship. Secondly the study on the impact on tourism exposed a significant collusive and negligent approach by consultants involved in ESIA. The Vizhinjam port project as a result of being subject to EIA regulations of the Central Ministry of Environment and Forests engaged MOEF Accredited consultants to undertake the EIA. Within the stages of EIA, in 2004 a Techno Feasibility Study by L&T Rambol committed a site selection to the port. Various false data including the impact on number of resorts was used by L&T. Significantly L&T stated that only 3 resorts exist in Vizhinjam and Poovar. The Consultants engaged later in 2009 included the International Finance Corporation, Royal Haskoning and Asian Consulting Engineers. ACE is an MOEF Accredited Consultant as well. Environmental Scoping was conducted by the these consultants under the coordination of the International Finance Corporation in 2010 that engaged filed visits and Environmental Scoping to be compliant with MOEF and IFC norms. The task of the IFC, RH and ACE was however, limited to the study of the site in Vizhinjam alone. In as late as August 2010, the Environmental Scoping Report by Asian Consulting Engineers, International Finance Corporation and Royal Haskoning falsely highlighted specifically that only 3 resorts would be affected by the Vizhinjam Port. This specific misinformation was transmitted to the MOEF Expert Committee on CRZ Projects who based the issuance of the Project's Terms of Reference on this incorrect data. It remains in poor light to the process of fairness, that thus far in EIA a separate report from the later consultants IFC, ACE and RH, who undertook field visits, stated once again that only 3 resorts would suffer perfectly in conformity with what L&T Rambol stated.

The quality and extent of studies conducted, when compared with data received under Right to Information, show that several key aspects of the EIA and Decision Making stages were incomplete, ignored or incorrect. Apart from the incorrectness of the true extent of resorts directly affected, the areas lacking during site selection and issuance of terms of reference for the EIA Study included non completion of Shoreline impact studies, A serious study on the true extent of impact on Kovalam Beach that lies just 1.5 km from the proposed port. The misrepresentations on existence of endangered species in Vizhinjam and areas already subjected to illegally permissible pollution norms, stated misrepresentations on non existence of endangered species in Vizhinjam to the MOEF Committee were once again stated similarly in reports by L&T Rambol and the later set of 3 consultants—IFC, ACE and RH. These amounted to various aspects of the EIA Study being overlooked, especially the definition of the Study area which was in violation of MOEF Guidelines on applied from the project boundary and ought to have been for 15km in total as opposed to the 10 km currently used. In the truest sense, project development through the various Government policy systems resulted in a weak set of Terms of Reference being framed for an EIA study of socially significant risks. The need for an appropriate and technically valid EIA stems with top priority in the context of the two already existing thriving industries in Vizhinjam, namely, Fishing and Tourism.

If the initial projections and market study report predictions, undertaken for the Vizhinjam project are considered, the viability of the Port for the Public Exchequer is extremely low. In addition the debt burden associated with Construction Costs are never fully sustained by port revenues generated for the State under the Landlord Model. In port employment generated amounts to only about 500 in 30 years while the port itself entails a modest projected revenue stream on account of the dominance of Colombo, Tuticorin and perilous situation of Cochin Port. Studies from the International Finance Corporation highlight that major share of traffic expected is the rerouted traffic from Cochin Port. The NPV for the public sector under IFC analysis showed a value of merely 50 Crores as opposed to a projected expenditure of over 4,000 Crores for the State. The often mistakenly projected benefit of no maintenance dredging on account of low littoral drift is unfounded as Trivandrum District is among the MOEF recommended high shoreline change districts for EIA. Research data and established field data show the nature of beaches changing over the year evidencing significantly visible littoral drift of sea sand. Sea currents are active in maintaining the marine resource used for close shore fishing. In reality the port has an equal chance of being a complete failure as that of the Cochin Port, bogged by inefficiency and high costs. The estimations by IFC again point out that Transshipment does not have significant linkages to the local economy. The Vizhinjam Port in its current location has no usable hinterland and as a result will not stimulate industrial growth in the area. The densely populated hinterland is cliffy and often congested with fishing and tourism activities. This is likely to create conflicting social problems and increased resource scarcity from port, consumption of water and electricity. A road so far constructed, as part of the last mile connectivity to the port, has resulted in the water table of the Mulloor village to dry up considerably. The total destructive ecological impacts on the marine fishery resource is to be felt directly on a mussels fishing grounds for over 5000 traditional fishermen. Access issues and safety of fishing operations will remain challenged on account of the proximity to fishing harbour mouth and conflict with tourism activities. The existing fishing harbour due to this high littoral drift in the area is to likely experience siltation on account of the port breakwaters in proximity. Experts highlight that considering the fishing harbour, not commissioned even after 50 years of construction, being a precedent, will likely result in a port undertaken but never completed meaningfully for many decades. A constant stream of public resources is granted for development but the real costs are never calculated. The project if subjected to a Cost Benefit Analysis, as per MOEF and IFC Standards, will result in a severely negative outcome. The sheer value of investment into tourism in the area and value of fisheries for livelihoods, once factored into a meaningful Cost Benefit Analysis, highlights that the port is a negative on account of loss in public finances, social impacts, environmental impacts, fishery impacts, loss of jobs, loss and destruction of areas of outstanding natural beauty. The true risk reward ratio of this project is one that a responsible government would recognize as a direct function of its particular site selected as seen by a negative ERR in actuality. The potential for improvement in planning is evident if a new site selection is conducted to minimize costs, impacts and environmental impacts, thereby improving the chances of the project becoming successful.

The answer to satisficing entails a willingness to change by the Policy Makers once information is attained on valid accounts. The proposed port has no economic logic in its current location and will spell the end of fisheries and tourism in the Kovalam Vizhinjam Poovar belt. In addition to the misrepresentations and policy violations that mandate corrective action in the terms of reference for the EIA Study, the project is currently subject to a review by the Internal Ombudsman of the IFC for Due Diligence and Integrity, ESIA Impacts, Fishery Aspects, Tourism Aspects and loss of ground water in Mulloor as a result of the road constructed.